More Essex MURDERS

LINDA STRATMANN

The History Press

To Marcus,
one of the genuine good guys

First published 2011

The History Press
The Mill, Brimscombe Port
Stroud, Gloucestershire, GL5 2QG
www.thehistorypress.co.uk

British Library Cataloguing in Publication Data.
A catalogue record for this book is available from the British Library.

ISBN 978 0 7524 5850 2

Typesetting and origination by The History Press
Printed in Great Britain

Manufacturing managed by Jellyfish Print Solutions Ltd

CONTENTS

ACKNOWLEDGEMENTS

I would like to offer my grateful thanks to all the people who have been so generous with their time in assisting me in my research for this book.

I should especially mention Becky Wash of the Essex Police Museum for a very enjoyable visit and a tremendous amount of help with the illustrations, Duncan Ward for help with Leo Brown's family tree, Linda Dudman for help with Emma Read's family tree, Alec Hare of Walthamstow Cemetery for identifying the grave of George Stanley Grimshaw, Penny Stynes of Colchester Cemetery for her help in locating the grave of Mary Kriek, Christine Rhodes and June Lindsell for a wonderful tour of St Mary's Church, Widdington and identifying the grave of James Mumford.

I would like to thank everyone at the British Library, Colindale Newspaper Library and the National Archives for their patient help.

And this would not be a list of those to whom I am indebted without a mention of my husband Gary, who accepts unquestioningly my fascination with murder and is always there to support my writing.

1

IN A DARK
AND LONELY PLACE

Widdington, 1823

At 8.30 p.m. on Monday, 8 December 1823, Robert Smith, a publican of Poynders Hill, Birchanger, was riding his pony down a narrow, winding country lane with fields of wheat and turnips on either side. He had just left the Fleur de Lys public house, Widdington, a village 4 miles south of Saffron Walden, and was heading towards the turnpike at Quendon. There was a moon, but the sky was overcast – he later described the night as 'glum' – and he would only have been able to see a short distance ahead. About half a mile from Widdington, in the darkest part of the lane, flanked by thickly growing hedgerows, his pony shied at something in the road. He alighted, and discovered a man lying on the ground, semi-conscious and groaning, his clothing torn and disordered.

Smith helped the man to sit up and spoke to him, but there was no coherent answer, so he took him to the side of the road, and, convinced that a murderous attack had taken place, rode back to the Fleur de Lys to get help. The blood that soaked one side of his coat told its own story, and four men hurried to the scene with candles and lanterns. Smith ordered a horse and cart to follow, then rode on to report the incident. Accounts differ as to the person he intended to alert, but it was most likely John Haydon, a Widdington farmer who was the parish overseer. Haydon was not at home, and Smith quickly rode back to the lane.

Meanwhile, the search party, labourers Matthew Dellow and George Reed and carpenters John Reed and George Reed the younger, were approaching the scene of the attack, but they were by their own account, about thirty rods away (a rod is approximately 5 metres) when they heard someone cry 'Hoy!' They went on and were within three or four rods of the person when they recognised the tall muscular figure of twenty-one-year-old labourer John Pallett, who was walking towards them carrying the body of the injured man draped over his shoulder. 'Here is James Mumford!' said Pallett. Like many other men in the area, including John Reed, Pallett worked for yeoman farmer Thomas Mumford, who occupied Priors Hall, Widdington, a 300-acre holding which belonged to Brazenose College Oxford. Mumford had three sons, one of whom was twenty-three-year-old James, familiarly known as 'Jem'.

John Reed held a lantern up to the face of the unknown man, and the light revealed some appalling injuries. The victim had been attacked with such savagery that the back of his head was beaten in, and his jaw and facial bones crushed. His features were so swollen and disfigured that neither Reed nor any of his companions could recognise him. He was no longer groaning and appeared to be dead, but the ruined face was still oozing blood, which had saturated Pallett's smock-frock. Reed, who had known James Mumford for many years, was sure it was not he, and the others agreed, but Pallett, who carried no light with him, said he knew it was. When Reed asked how he knew, Pallett looked confused and simply repeated that he was certain. At this point, Robert Smith returned and the body was put into the cart and taken to Widdington. The limp figure was carried into the parlour of the Fleur de Lys, and placed in a chair. The landlady, Mrs Whisken, noticed some initials 'J.M.' marked on the man's shirt, and when John Reed recognised a mole on the battered cheek, he confirmed that Pallett had been right. James Mumford's mother, Mary, was sent for, and identified the body of her son.

Pallett, who was bloodied about the face, left the tap-room to wash, and in his absence there must have been some discussion about his unexpected appearance on the scene. He seemed to have appeared from nowhere within minutes, which suggested that he might have been lurking nearby, and the men wondered how he had known, despite the darkness and disfigurement, that the body was that of James Mumford. Pallett's family were known to be of good character. His father, fifty-three-year-old Thomas, worked for James Mumford's father, tending to his horses. However, young John, who had worked for the Mumfords since he was a child, had a bad reputation. He frequented fairs where he had sometimes caused riots, had on many occasions been found guilty of drunkenness and profane swearing, and was known to have a 'very malicious temper'. Pallett's misdemeanours had resulted in his being punished by James, who had impounded his pigs when he had trespassed on the Mumfords' lands, and lopped boughs from the trees, and James had also had him fined 5s for drunkenness. Although the punishments were deserved, they had given rise to intense hatred and resentment and Pallett had been heard to threaten that he would 'do' for 'Jem Mumford'.

At 10 p.m. that evening, Parish Constable George Knight arrived, and when John Reed told him how they had found Pallett carrying the body, he decided to take Pallett into custody. At first the prisoner submitted quietly, but then took violent exception to being handcuffed, and there was a struggle during which Pallett knocked over a table, breaking plates and glasses. Knight called out for assistance and seven or eight men came to help the constable subdue the prisoner. Eventually, Pallett was secured, threatening that he would smash them all. They were obliged to tie up his legs to stop him kicking out.

Hollow Lane, formerley Quendon Want Lane, site of the murder of James Mumford.

According to local legend, the body of James Mumford was placed in this corner of the Fleur de Lys public house. (Picture by kind permission of the landord)

James Mumford from a contemporary print. (By kind permission of Gary Dunnett)

Pallett was searched, and in his right-hand breeches pocket was found a knife which had two notches on its blade. There was also a comb, and 2*s* and four pence in a canvas purse. In the left-hand pocket was a knife with a buck-horn handle, and Knight recognised it as one he had often seen in the possession of James Mumford.

That Monday, James Mumford had been visiting his brother George in Smithfield, London, who was apprenticed to a Mr Burbidge at 127 St John Street. James was near sighted, and had bought some new spectacles in a red morocco case. He had left London by the Saffron Walden coach at 2 p.m., carrying with him his new spectacles and his buck-horn-handled knife. The coach reached Quendon at 7.30 p.m., arriving at the Coach and Horses public house with James Mumford sitting on the box above. Thomas Kidman, a huckster of Newport, had been selling oysters at the Coach and Horses, and drinking there since about 4 p.m. with John Pallett and another man, and between them they had consumed about twelve pints of beer.

As the coach drew up, Pallett was standing at the door and saw it arrive. The coach did not pass through Widdington, and the driver, addressing Mumford by name, asked him if his luggage was to be left at the Coach and Horses or taken to his house. Mumford said that his luggage was to remain at the Coach and Horses, and he would send for it later. He intended to ride in the coach as far as the Quendon turnpike, about three quarters of a mile away, where the road forked and the coach went on to Saffron Walden. There he would alight and take the lane, known at that point as Quendon Want Lane, walking to Widdington alone.

As the coach set off again, Pallett and Kidman left the Coach and Horses together, taking with them Kidman's donkey and following the coach, walking at a good pace. William Dellow, the ostler at the Coach and Horses, rode with the coach as far as the turnpike, and passed Pallett and Kidman, but as the coach rattled past them they picked up their speed, Pallett riding the donkey and Kidman running, following on almost as fast as the coach for about twenty rods. He lost sight of them about a quarter of a mile from the turnpike.

It was a few minutes to eight when George Say, son of the turnpike keeper at Quendon, saw the coach halt and James Mumford get down. Mumford borrowed an elm switch from Say to help him feel his way along the dark road, and set off for the mile-and-a-half walk home. Pallett and Kidman were not far behind. As they approached the turnpike, Pallett jumped off the donkey and the two men decided to go their separate ways, but not before Pallett had borrowed Kidman's knife. Five or six minutes after the coach had passed through, George Say saw Kidman riding his donkey through the gate on the road to Saffron Walden. Pallett was not with him.

John Pallett, the main suspect for the murder of James Mumford, had to remain at the Fleur de Lys overnight until he could be removed to a secure lock-up. The constable sat up with him, but at the request of Thomas Mumford Jnr, one of the dead man's brothers, he removed the prisoner's shoes. They were countryman's 'high shoes' or 'half-boots', with thick nails in the soles, and it was hoped they would be found to match shoeprints found at the scene of the crime.

At midnight, John Haydon, who had by then heard the alarm, went out with two others to make a candlelight search of the road where the body was found. He discovered a great deal of blood running down the cart tracks in the road, a pair of gloves and a little elm switch.

The next morning he searched again, and in a field of turnips he found a thick hazel stick, about 26in long, which appeared to have been cut with a notched knife. It was heavily stained with blood and one end was split as if it had been used for repeated blows. About fifteen rods further on he found a hat and coat, some keys, another knife, a pencil case and a pair of spectacles in a red morocco case. The hat was much bloodied and cut across the crown. All these items were delivered to the constable.

The Fleur de Lys, 2010. (By kind permission of the landlord)

That morning, James' brother John was given the prisoner's shoes to compare with footprints near the scene of the crime. When John Pallett, still chained up in the Fleur de Lys, saw Mumford going past the window he asked where he was going and, on learning what was proposed, exclaimed, 'Then I shall be sure to be done: it is a hard thing to be born to be hung...'. Pallett was later taken to the house of correction in Newport, crying out all the way that he was sure to hang.

John Mumford made a careful examination of the wheat field. A great many of the murderer's footprints had been obliterated by the trampling feet of searchers, but he was able to follow a track starting three or four rods from the blood in the road of what appeared to be running feet. After twelve rods he found a place on a ridge of wheat where there was a mark as if someone had sat down there, and beside it were two holes which looked as if a split stick had been stuck in the ground. The same footsteps then went towards the adjoining field of turnips to where Haydon had found the murdered man's property. John Mumford began comparing the prisoner's high shoes with the footmarks, starting from those nearest the blood, following them from there to the seat in the ground, then on to where the coat and other things were found, and thence back towards the lane. He compared them in over a hundred places, and found that they corresponded. He also saw that in two instances the person who had crossed the turnip field had trodden on some turnips and made marks which exactly corresponded with nails in the toes of the shoes. The split hazel stick exactly fitted the two holes beside the seat in the wheat field.

John, aware that the hazel stick had been cut with a notched knife and that a knife of that description had been found on the prisoner, was determined to find the place where the murder weapon had been cut and instructed labourer James Franklin to examine all the hedges in the neighbourhood. Near the turning from Quendon to Widdington were hazel trees cut down to stumps, known as stools, from which new growth would arise, and it was found that a piece had been freshly cut from a stool using a notched knife. Franklin removed the piece of stool from which the stick had been cut. The stool and the murder weapon were then compared and they were a match.

That Tuesday morning, Mr George Eachus, a surgeon of Saffron Walden, saw the body. He found a lacerated wound on the lower side of the left jaw, which looked as though it had been caused by a blow with a stick. Every bone in the skull apart from the frontal bone was fractured. On one side, a piece of bone the size of his hand was loose and he was able to remove it, while on the other side the skull was 'shivered to pieces'. He later stated that the injuries were 'sufficient to have killed a thousand men.'

On the same day, John Pallett was brought to Saffron Walden to be questioned. Thomas Hall, clerk to the magistrates of Saffron Walden, took the depositions of the witnesses which were read over to the prisoner. He was asked if he had anything to say and replied 'Nothing'. The buckhorn-handled knife was shown to him, and he claimed to have found it in Baggot Field, Widdington, about a fortnight before. He was remanded until the result of the inquest was known.

The inquest was held at the Fleur de Lys on Thursday 11 December, and Pallett arrived by cart, handcuffed and with heavy irons on both legs. He was confined to an ante-room and during the proceedings, which took five and a half hours, he was several times so overcome with emotion that he fainted. The jury went to view the body, which had been taken to James' father's house, and, after hearing the evidence, returned a verdict of wilful murder against John Pallett. The Coroner committed him for trial and ordered that he be taken to Chelmsford Gaol. That same evening a Mr Brodrick was retained to conduct the prosecution on behalf of the Crown.

As he travelled to the gaol by cart, Pallett asked to be allowed to speak to Thomas Hall. The cart stopped at the Saracen's Head Inn, where Hall was staying, and a message was sent to Hall. The clerk had not seen Pallett since recording the depositions on Tuesday, and knew that the magistrate, Mr Lodden, had cautioned the prisoner as to the effect of anything he might say. He emerged from the inn and approached the cart, where Pallett, speaking in a voice so low that Hall could scarcely understand him, asked Hall to get into the cart so they could talk. Pallett said that Kidman had given him the knife which he had used to cut the hazel stick. Hall asked him if Kidman had anything to do with the murder and Pallett answered, 'No, I alone did it.'

Pallett confirmed that on the night of the murder he had heard Mumford's name mentioned when the Saffron Walden coach arrived, and had gone to cut the stake specifically for the purpose of taking his revenge. He had easily overtaken Mumford, who had been slowly feeling his way down the dark lane with the elm switch, and was about to strike the fatal blow when his courage failed him. Mumford thought he heard someone nearby, but unable to see who it was, called out 'Who's there?' in a tone of alarm. Pallett said nothing and stood still, holding his breath. Mumford again went on, and Pallett took a shortcut through a field to get in front of him, and

The Old Gaol, Moulsham Street, c.1820.

Portrait of John Pallett from a contemporary pamphlet.

THE
TRIAL and PORTRAIT
OF
JOHN PALLETT,

FROM A DRAWING
BY MRS. HAMILTON,
TAKEN FROM A CAST
BY *Mr. BERRY, OF CHELMSFORD,*
PLASTERER.

stood by a gate ready to strike. Again, his courage failed him and he did nothing. Mumford walked on and Pallett followed, and finally struck him on the head, knocking off his hat. Mumford staggered and Pallett struck again, felling his victim to the ground. He then rained repeated blows onto the head of the fallen man. His vengeance over, he retreated a short distance away, intending to make his escape, but suddenly conscious of what he had done, he found himself rooted to the spot, unable to move in any direction, staring at the body. He remained there until Smith arrived, and saw him approach the body and ride away but still he could not move. Once again he tried to escape, but was unable to resist the impulse to return to the body, and unsure of exactly what to do he picked it up, and threw it over his shoulder and was carrying it when the men arrived from Widdington.

Despite the terrible nature of the crime, Pallett was not without sympathetic friends. Some charitably minded people alerted to the fact that the defendant, the son of a poor cottager, had only 2s 4d to his name and believing that every man should be entitled to the best possible representation, started a subscription to enable him to obtain legal advice.

On Friday 12 December, a Mr Jessop was retained to conduct the defence, and on the following morning, less than five days after the crime was committed, the trial of John Pallett opened at Chelmsford Assizes. Long before nine o'clock, the hour appointed for the start of the trial, every vacant seat was occupied, and observers noticed that the gallery especially was filled by 'the fair sex' who took a particular interest in the proceedings.

The judge was sixty-year-old Sir James Alan Park; a man unafraid to express his firmly held opinions. He took his place on the bench punctually at nine, and before the prisoner was brought in, addressed the court. He had read in that morning's London newspapers the full details of the evidence given at the inquest. He took the strongest possible objection to their publication, and made his displeasure very plain in the following statement:

> I cannot but express my surprise that persons possessing the common feelings of humanity should thus take pains to increase the hazard of individuals who are going to take their trials...no human being but the Coroner has a right to take down the evidence...

Pallett was charged with the wilful murder of James Mumford, 'with a certain stick, of the value of three pence, with which he inflicted on his head divers mortal fractures.' During his stay in gaol, he had been attended by the chaplain, the Revd Mr Hutchinson, who had 'succeeded in awakening in his mind a proper sense of his situation' and found him willing to receive religious consolation. Hutchinson soon discovered that he had a blank slate to work with. Not only was Pallett completely illiterate, it was discovered with some astonishment that though the prisoner had frequented his parish church he was unable even to recite one sentence of the Lord's Prayer.

Pallett, brought to the bar wearing his smock-frock, waistcoat and a spotted handkerchief, was loaded with heavy irons and moved with difficulty. He looked deeply depressed and had lost much of his defiant spirit. He pleaded not guilty in a low voice, and spent much of the trial with his head held down.

Before the proceedings commenced, Mr Jessop rose to request that the trial should be postponed until the next assizes. He pointed out that the prisoner had only been committed to the gaol on Thursday night between 11 and 12 o'clock, having been brought from 25 miles away and unable to have access to anyone whose testimony might be essential to his defence. Jessop also referred to the publication of the evidence against the prisoner in the London newspapers, which had been circulated in Chelmsford, and could have been seen by the jury by whom he was to be tried, 'which could not but prejudice the minds of the jury upon the merits of the case.'

Mr Justice Park was not to be moved. 'I am clearly of the opinion that there is no ground for putting off this trial,' he said, adding that there was 'scarcely an assize paper in which forty or fifty persons are not put upon their trial for felonies, within a few hours of their commitment.' Referring to a case of 'one of the foulest murders which was ever committed in this kingdom', in which the murderer had been apprehended on a Monday and was executed on the following Monday, he commented, 'There is nothing at all extraordinary in such a proceeding.' Regarding the publication of the evidence, even though this was improper, the facts had not been accompanied by any comments. Even if this were an objection, the longer the trial was postponed the

Title page of a contemporary pamphlet about the trial of John Pallett.

THE

TRIAL

OF

JOHN PALLETT,

FOR THE

WILFUL MURDER

OF

MR. JAMES MUMFORD,

A respectable Farmer,

AT WIDDINGTON,

IN THE

COUNTY OF ESSEX,

AT

The Special Session of Gaol Delivery,

HOLDEN

AT CHELMSFORD,

ON SATURDAY MORNING,

The 13th Day of December, 1823,

BEFORE

MR. JUSTICE PARK.

MEGGY AND CHALK, PRINTERS,
CHELMSFORD.

more the evil complained of might be extended. 'Speedy justice, in my opinion, is one of the best preventives of crime.' He thus refused the application and the trial commenced.

Mr Brodrick opened the case for the Crown, urging the jury to dismiss from their minds any preconceived opinions they might have formed from reports or statements in 'the public papers.' He felt certain that 'their judgement would be the result of calm, dispassionate, and temperate consideration.' He then called his witnesses.

As George Knight gave his testimony, Pallett suddenly appeared to be faint, perhaps from the heat and the weight of his irons, or feelings of despair, and leaned forward on the bar. Mr Justice Park showed the humane nature that lay beneath the firm exterior by instructing that the prisoner should be given a glass of water and provided with a seat. Pallett was not the only one to be affected. As James Franklin gave his evidence, and the bloodstained hazel stick was brought before the court, one of James' bothers – probably the more emotional George – sobbed with grief.

The other articles found at the spot were produced by the constable, and the court saw that the dark brown coat was covered in dirt and smothered in blood. The hat was bloody inside and there was a hole in the top. John Mumford could not swear positively that the coat and hat were his brother's, although he knew Jem had a coat of that colour. The knife found in the field he recognised as one he had made a present of to his brother about six weeks before his death.

George Mumford was called and 'in an agony of grief' took the oath. Some time elapsed before he was able to give evidence, and when he did so he cried almost continuously. Looking at the buckhorn-handled knife found on the prisoner, he swore that it was his brother's. He also identified the spectacles in their morocco case.

There was evidence of the prisoner's antagonism towards Mumford. John Cock, a weaver of Saffron Walden, had been at the Queen's Head public house on the last Petty Sessions day, 22 November. He had gone in with a neighbour and seen Pallett and three other men there together drinking. 'Damn you, Cock,' said Pallett (Cock did not reveal if this was a usual greeting), 'will you drink?' Cock replied that 'he must mind and not get drunk.' Pallett warmed to his theme. 'We have got to pay for getting drunk,' he said. Cock asked him who wanted them to pay for getting drunk.' 'Little Jem Mumford,' said Pallett, 'a b****** (the trial transcript omitted to print the full expletive although *The Times* politely printed 'rascal')' adding that if he had him here, 'he'd smash him; but he'd be d****d if he would not be his match.' The other men then went away and Pallett revealed that they had been at the Sessions that day having been accused of drunkenness by James Mumford, and had been fined.

Susan Reed, the wife of John Reed of Widdington, told the court that about a fortnight ago she had heard Pallett say, 'I shouldn't mind hacking Jem Mumford's whistle,' by which she understood to mean that he would cut Mumford's throat. Neither she nor John Cock were asked if they had taken these threats seriously, and it seems probable that it was common for Pallett to talk in this way, especially when he had been drinking.

Thomas Hall told the court of Pallett's admission of sole guilt to him, and Kidman was shown the notched knife and said that it was his and he had lent it to Pallett shortly before the murder.

There were no witnesses for the defence. Mr Justice Park summed up the evidence and the jury took only a few minutes to return a verdict of guilty. Pallett stood up, supporting his irons in his hand, his head bowed low as if in shame. He was asked if he had anything to say, but remained silent. Park, whose voice was occasionally choked with emotion, pronounced sentence of death, decreeing that after the prisoner was dead his body 'be afterwards taken down and delivered to the surgeons to be dissected and anatomized'. Many people in court sobbed openly. Pallett seemed less moved and was heard to say only that he didn't mind dying if only Kidman were to die with him. The execution was set for Monday 15 December.

James Mumford was buried on Sunday, 14 December 1823 in Widdington churchyard.

On 15 December the editor of *The Times* taking objection to the suggestion that newspaper reports would exert undue influence on a jury, commented angrily on, '...the repetition of a doctrine so essentially erroneous and unreasonable...', pointing out that the jurors must inevitably know that the inquest had brought in a verdict of murder and the publication of the reasons was 'more favourable to truth and justice than the circulation of loose and colloquial tales...'

John Pallett's last night on earth was a restful one. He went to bed at 1.30 a.m. and slept soundly until 6 a.m. He was then awoken, but fell fast asleep again. The place of execution lay between the gaol and the river, and was shut off by a high wall in front, with a gate through which spectators were admitted. As soon as the light of day dawned, it was seen that the wall immediately above the place where

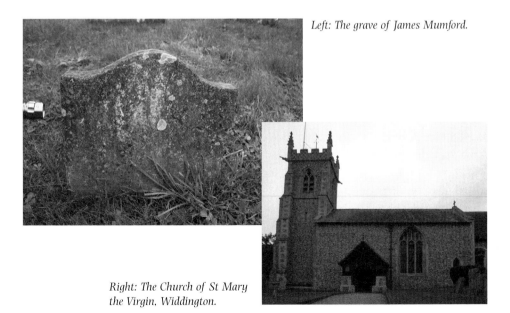

Left: The grave of James Mumford.

Right: The Church of St Mary the Virgin, Widdington.

15

A full and particular Account of the Trial and

EXECUTION

Of JOHN PALLET, which took place at Chelmsford, on Monday last, Dec. 15th, 1823, for the cruel and barbarous

MURDER

Of Mr James Mumford, on Monday Dec. 8th, near Widdington, in Essex : with a full Account of his Behaviour at the Place of Execution.

JOHN PALLET was young, strong, and idle, he was uneducated, and he had no better idea of character than an ox that grazeth in the field. On Monday, Dec. 8, 1823. this young man committed this inhuman murder, from no motive of plunder but from sheer malice, the deceased had pounded his pigs, and had him fined 5s. for being drunk on a Sunday. He was drinking at a public house, when Mr James Mumford went past the window, and according to his own confession, he followed him down the lane, and cut a stick from the hedge; but when he overtook him, his heart failed him twice, he then went over the hedge and ran and got before him, and in an instant felled him to the ground, and struck him to that degree that his head was flat, and no one could know him. He then left him and went into a field, when a Mr Smith rode up, and saw the body, he immediately rode back to the public-house, and sent the men who were drinking, to fetch it, when they met the Prisoner with the body on his back, with the head downwards and legs over his shoulders he immediately told them it was James Mumford, and accompanied them to the public house when he immediately began to drink. No one could know the body, and they asked Pallet how he knew it was James Mumford? Which confused him very much. They immediately seized him and it took six men to secure him, a knife of the deceased was found in his waistcoat pocket. He was sent to gaol to take his trial at the assizes which were then going on.

He was tried on Friday before Mr Justice Park, and fully convicted of this horrid Murder, and sentenced to be hung on Monday.

On Saturday he felt none of the agitations of a man distracted between hope and fear : he never immagined escape possible and heard the sentence unmoved, and slept soundly till the last.

Monday Dec. 15, this day week John

Pallet was an innocent man, and now he is a corpse, for the foulest murder that can be conceived in immagination. The shortness of time for such a transition is very striking. The place of execution is an open space between the gaol and the river, about half past seven o'clock in the morning six young men arrived there weeping most bitterly. One of them the brother of the culprit, fixed an ardent gaze on the platform, the rest turned their backs to the agonizing scene, and cried aloud. At the end of 5 minutes they quietly withdrew. He went to bed the night before at 12 o'clock and slept soundly till about 6 o'clock in the morning, when he was awoke, and actually fell fast asleep again. His ignorance exceeded belief. The parting with his relations was truly distressing, and his father and mother are not expected to live.

At a quarter past 9 the chaplain took leave of him. He was then pinioned and bound hard by the rists, all the while he kept crying and muttering "Lord help me." He moved slowly from the stage to the platform bare headed, and with his large fair neck exposed. His visage upon stepping from the outer gate, was dreadfully expressive, his upper lip was partially drawn up in the agony of despair. His large toilmarked hands were swolen and livid with the tightness of his bandages, his half boots were dirty and unlaced. The smock frock bearing the mark of the blood of the murdered Mumford. He ascended the Platform very slowly but firmly. The instant he was placed in the station for execution he glanced at the crowd, the executioner covered his head and face with a cap, when this opperation began, he groaned with most affecting energy, and he continued for some time rising slowly on his tip-toes, and falling strongly back on his heels, the executioner having adjusted the rope, the platform fell, and he was launched into eternity. He struggled much and the executioner pulled at his feet till he died.

W. Stephenson, Printer, Gateshead.

A contemporary account of the trial and execution of John Pallett.

the platform was to be raised had been covered with a black cloth. By then many people were already assembled on the bridge to view the preparations. At half past seven a number of young men arrived, all relatives – most probably brothers – of the murdered man, weeping bitterly with convulsive sobs. One brother gradually became more composed, and fixed his eyes steadily on the spot, while the others wept aloud and turned their backs on the scene. After five minutes of contemplation they departed.

At half past eight the gates were thrown open and the crowd surged in. A temporary defence had been set across the ground a few feet from the platform and the people thronged densely right up to the barrier. In the prison Pallett's irons were struck off and he walked firmly and slowly to the chapel, where he received the sacrament. The chaplain took his leave of him at a quarter past nine and the prisoner was then bound hard by the wrists. As this was done he moaned and occasionally muttered, 'Lord help me!'

When he stepped from the passage to the outer ground, it was seen that his upper lip was drawn back in a grimace of despair, his eyes mournful. His hands, large and marked with toil, were swollen and livid with the tightness of the bindings. He was still wearing the clothes in which he had been arrested, his boots were dirty and unlaced, and his smock-frock still bore on the left breast and shoulder the marks of Mumford's blood, where he had flung the body as he lifted it. Slowly but firmly he ascended the platform, where the executioner was waiting. He glanced round at the expectant crowd, but almost immediately the executioner covered his face with a nightcap and then bound a handkerchief over his eyes, Pallett groaning all the while, and repeatedly rising up on his toes then falling back on his heels.

The executioner took a long time to adjust the rope, and then shook Pallett strongly by his clasped hands. The steps were removed, and then the platform, which was attached permanently by hinges to the wall and was being supported by a locked spring, was dropped. It was a short drop and the prisoner would, without assistance, have slowly strangled to death, but the executioner held on to Pallett's legs to speed the process until he was dead. The crowd watched in awed silence, but not, it was thought, with any feelings of sympathy.

After his death, Pallett's confession was published:

I had been drinking with Kidman as the Coach and Horses, Quendon, all the afternoon, and was somewhat inflamed with the liquor I had drank. From this place we both started with the intent of going to Newport to get sand. I was riding on Kidman's donkey and he was beating it with his oyster measure. When we came to opposite Quendon Want-lane we observed someone go down. Kidman went forward to see who it was, and on his return said 'It's Jem Mumford' Kidman then lent me his knife to cut a stick, and I said 'D**n him he shall have it.' I then got off the donkey and followed Mumford down the lane. Kidman left me and proceeded through the turnpike. I overtook Mr Mumford upon a hill, without his perceiving me, and struck him a blow on the head; but he did not fall from the first blow; I think I struck him again, and he fell. When down I repeated the blows with the stick until he was incapable of resistance. Having done so, I felt in his pockets and took out the knife, which betrayed me, and put it into my own pocket.

Mr Mumford had his great coat upon his arm, which I took, and also several small things which I do not recollect: these I carried into the turnip field adjoining. I then sat down upon a piece of wheat, and stuck the stick into the ground by my side. I began to reflect; for it was not my intention, at first, to have committed murder but only to beat him severely; and I placed my two hands upon my face, saying to myself 'Good God!

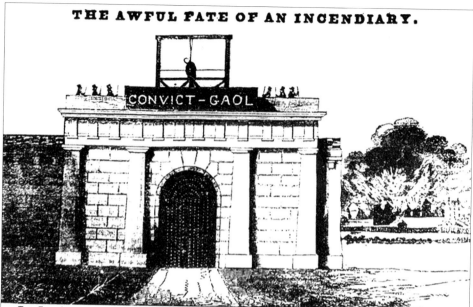

THE AWFUL FATE OF AN INCENDIARY.

CONVICT-GAOL

This Engraving represents the Entrance of the County of Essex Convict Gaol—the Place of Execution on the Morning of the 27th of March, 1829, when James Cook, a boy only 16 years of age, suffered for the atrocious crime of setting on fire the premises of Mr. William Green, of Witham, farmer, with whom he lived as Cow Boy.

The Buildings and Stacks, which are represented as burning, furnish a true picture of the lamentable destruction of property occasioned by this wicked boy.

It is a melancholy fact, that there are offenders of the same cast still abroad, who by their conduct, show, that the disgraceful end of Cook has not operated as a sufficient example, to deter them from the commission of the like heinous crime; such, however, may be assured, that justice will ultimately overtake and punish them.

A hanging at Chelmsford Gaol in 1829.

What have I been doing?' About this time I heard the footsteps of a horse; he stopped at the spot where I left Mr Mumford, and shortly after I heard the horse return. I then returned to the body, forgetting that I had put the knife in my pocket; I kneeled down upon one knee, and raised Mr Mumford, and sat him upon the other, and rested his chin upon my left shoulder, when the blood poured down my neck in torrents, and made the collar of my shirt in the state it was in when the persons came up. I next took the body on my back, and proceeded on my way to Widdington, under the impression that I should be able to convince the family that I found him, and was performing a friendly office. In my way I was met by four men, and soon after a cart came.

When I came to the public-house I placed the body on a chair, but it fell, and I endeavoured to place it there again. Mrs Whisken, the landlady of the public-house, found a mark upon Mr Mumford's shirt, which satisfied those present it was Jem Mumford. I then left the room to wash the blood from my face, which I did as well as I could, and afterwards returned to the tap-room, where, shortly after, I was taken into custody.

Nowadays, the lane where James Mumford was killed is known as Hollow Lane, but it still retains the same lonely atmosphere it had in 1823.

2

THE MILDNESS
OF MURDERERS

Doddinghurst, 1850

In 1850 the quiet and secluded village of Doddinghurst, consisting of a few farming homesteads and labourers' cottages, suddenly found itself at the centre of a murder case which horrified the county of Essex. The village lies in a valley, served by the River Wid and its tributaries, and is connected by a winding road leading three miles south to Brentwood.

Twenty-three-year-old Thomas Drory was the son of James, one of the most respected inhabitants of Little Burstead about 3 miles east of Brentwood, where he farmed a substantial holding. James also owned Brickhouse Farm near Canterbury Tye Hall on the Doddinghurst road, the two farms together comprising 355 acres and employing nine labourers. Thomas managed the Doddinghurst farm for his father, tending to the pigs, fowls and calves, milking cows, taking goods into the village and to Brentwood to sell, and working in the fields. He was regarded by his neighbours as, 'a young man of the most steady and persevering business habits,' although some said that 'he did not appear to possess that amount of keenness and sagacity which young farmers nowadays lay claim to.' This was a mild criticism indeed, and Thomas was not known for the more serious vices of drunkenness, dishonesty or violence. A slightly built young man with a trim, active figure, and 5ft 6in tall, he was fair haired, and good-looking with small, delicate, almost feminine features, and a florid open-air complexion.

The Drory's bailiff, sixty-five-year-old Thomas Last, had, since the summer of 1848, lived at Brickhouse Farm together with his wife Louisa, who acted as housekeeper. Louisa had four children by a prior marriage, one of whom, Jael Denny, was born on 13 June 1830. Jael, with 'a remarkably fine figure and prepossessing features', was a strong, well proportioned young woman, standing 5ft 9in in height. She was said to have a 'ladylike demeanour' and dressed neatly but not smartly, as she was often short of money. Jael had gone into domestic service, and her parents sometimes had to help her financially when she was out of work. She had her admirers – farm labourer Aaron Byatt had promised her marriage and it was rumoured that a tailor called Hubbard had also wanted to marry her, but Jael had a better prospect – Thomas Drory.

Jael and Thomas saw each other often and, by the spring of 1849, the flirtation had become an affair. Jael might have hoped that Thomas would marry her, which would be a substantial boost both to her social status and fortunes, but Thomas, who may well have hinted at marriage as part of his seduction technique, had no intention of marrying his servant's daughter. When James Drory learned of the liaison he ordered Jael to leave Brickhouse Farm, and she was obliged to find lodgings, where Thomas, probably without the knowledge of his father, would call upon her two or three times a week.

By April 1850 Jael must have realised that she was pregnant. She was lodging in South Weald with a widow, Susan Twinn, to whom she confided that Thomas's friends disapproved of his associating with her. Susan, convinced that Jael's relationship with Thomas could only end badly, told him to keep away, but the couple continued to meet, although after April, less frequently. Jael stayed with Susan until 11 July and concealed her condition so well that her landlady never suspected that she was pregnant. Jael then went to lodge with George and Mary Wheal of Blackmore, and as the summer progressed it became increasingly apparent that she had excellent prospects of carrying the child to a healthy term and that Drory did not want to marry her.

On a visit to Brickhouse Farm that summer (the date is unknown), Louisa noticed that Jael's lips and nose were swollen. The girl was ill and faint, agitated, unable to eat and her breath smelt. Jael confessed that Thomas had given her something to take and she had swallowed some of it. When her face swelled she realised that whatever he had given her was poisonous and thought if she had taken it all it would have killed her. 'He is a naughty boy,' said Jael, adding that she had put the rest of the poison onto the fire. Louisa commented that she wondered that anyone would let Thomas have poison.

It was not until Jael visited the farm on 3 September that she told her mother that she was expecting a child which was due in two months. Thomas also had a visitor that day, Joseph Giblin, the son of a farmer and corn-dealer of South Weald, with a twenty-year-old sister, Clarissa. Louisa confronted Thomas with Jael's condition, at which young Giblin looked from Jael to Thomas and grinned. Louisa was incensed. 'What did you see to grin at? For my part I see nothing to grin at.' She turned to Drory. 'Thomas,' she said, 'You must be a villain. I know you are going to be married to Miss Giblin, and my daughter is seven months gone in the family way by you.' Drory made no reply, but when Louisa continued to task him about it over the next few days he denied that Jael's child was his. Thomas Last also tried speaking to Drory about Jael's pregnancy, but the young man would not discuss it.

It was probably this development at Brickhouse Farm which resulted in James Drory giving Thomas and Louisa notice to quit. On 28 September 1850 they moved to a cottage half a mile away on Cumber's Farm, and were joined there by Jael.

A new bailiff and housekeeper moved into Brickhouse Farm; William Stone Hubbard and his wife Susannah.

Despite everything, Jael was looking forward to the birth of her child. She said she hoped the child would live, and planned to go out to work as soon as she could to support it. The usual requisites for a lying-in were prepared, a midwife was engaged, and it was agreed that Louisa would nurse her daughter after the birth. Jael's pregnancy was now the talk of the village especially as she made no secret of the fact that Thomas Drory was responsible.

As her confinement drew near, Jael asked Thomas for money, which he promised her (the sum of £10 was rumoured), but on one condition – he wanted Jael to disown all connection with him. On 29 September Louisa and her husband returned briefly to the farm to collect some fruit trees they had left behind, Jael remaining alone in the cottage. Drory had been in the garden with his brother Benjamin, but Louisa suddenly noticed that he had gone. When she returned home, she found Jael downstairs looking 'hot and trembling.' 'What is the matter with you?' demanded Louisa, but Jael only said, 'I will tell you by and by.' Going upstairs, Louisa found Thomas Drory hiding underneath her bed. He got up and handed her a paper – asking if she would sign it. It was a statement in Jael's handwriting. Dated that day it read:

> This is to prove that the trouble I am in is not by Thomas Drory, although I suppose it has been reported it is, and therefore I wish to satisfy the minds of those who may read this note, that I wish them to trouble themselves about their own business.

Louisa refused to sign the paper and went downstairs. 'What a fool you are,' she said to her daughter. 'You must be a fool to flurry yourself and write a pack of nonsense just to please him.' Jael said nothing, but later told her mother that Thomas had pleaded that if she had any love for him, she would write a note which he promised he would only show to Miss Giblin.

On 1 October, Thomas Drory was ploughing a field and discussing a recent sale with George Nichols, a market gardener of South Weald. Drory was angry with another market gardener, William Hammond, 'for scandalising his character at the sale', and told Nichols about the paper Jael had written, adding, 'George, you will hear something very serious of her some time, for she told me on Sunday morning that she would make away with herself.' 'I hope you don't think so, Thomas,' said Nichols, but Drory asserted that Jael had told him this two or three times. He was so overwrought that he set in his plough at the wrong end of the field and confessed that he was 'sure he did not know what he was about.'

On the afternoon of Saturday 12 October, Jael was only two weeks from her confinement. She wanted to speak to Thomas and went out between 4 and 5 p.m. to see if she could find him. She was not gone long, and on her return told her mother that she had found Thomas and walked and talked with him. 'How did he behave?' asked Louisa. 'Very well indeed, mother,' replied Jael, 'and he has put me in quite good spirits; he has appointed to meet me again at half past six, and I want to be exact in time, because he told me he was going out.' Louisa made the family tea and they all sat down together. The meal was not yet finished when Jael looked at the clock, put her bread and butter down, got up, and said, 'I will finish my tea when I come back; I shall not be gone long, I am only going to the first stile in the mead.' It was a cold day and Jael tied a cloth about her face to ward off toothache, put on a cloak and bonnet and went out, 'full of cheerful spirits.' Shortly afterwards she was seen in the company of Thomas Drory walking over some meadows away from the village.

Louisa waited for Jael to come home and finish off her bread and butter but her daughter never returned. Mr and Mrs Last waited up for Jael in anxious suspense until 11 p.m. Shortly after 5 a.m. the following morning, afraid that Jael had come to harm at the hands of Thomas Drory, they went out to search, taking different directions. Louisa went to Brickhouse Farm to see Drory, who was busy milking the cows. She asked where her daughter was and he replied that he didn't know as he hadn't seen her. Louisa retorted that that was untrue as he had seen Jael the day before between 4 and 5 p.m. and made an appointment to see her again at 6.30 p.m. She demanded to know where he had left her but he said he had not seen her after 5 p.m. and had gone to Brentwood.

Thomas Last, meanwhile, had checked the river, the ponds on the adjacent farms, and peered into a well, but found nothing, and at eight o'clock he was on his way home. He was passing through a meadow known as the 'Seven Acre Field' or 'Mr Cumber's Mead' not far from his cottage, when he saw what he thought was an ox lying in the grass in a secluded area shaded by a thick clump of trees, close to where a rivulet marked the boundary of the parishes of Doddinghurst and Shenfield. Approaching, he saw that it was the body of his daughter, lying face down, clothed exactly as she had been when she left home. It was only a quarter of a mile from the stile where Jael had said she was to meet Thomas Drory. A cord was wound tightly about her neck and it was obvious that she was dead. Her right hand lay under her, her left hand, which was bent back, loosely clasping one end of the cord. Last ran towards his cottage, his moans of distress attracting the attention of William Hammond, whose house was nearby, and who accompanied him back to the body. When they lifted Jael they saw that her face was dark and swollen, her mouth bloody, the tongue protruding and clenched tightly by the teeth. Blood oozed from her nose, eyes and ears. The body was still warm although her arms and legs were cold and stiff.

Hammond left Last with the body and went straight to Drory's house where he learned that immediately after breakfast Drory had gone with a basket of apples to see a farmer, Robert Moore, at Shenfield. Hammond then reported what he knew to Superintendent Thomas Coulson at Brentwood police station. Coulson, accompanied by Constable William Lenan, went to Robert Moore's farm, where he found Drory seated at the fire, clad in a fustian jacket, corduroy breeches and leather gaiters. Drory said that he had last seen Jael at 5 p.m. the previous evening, but denied having made any later appointment with her and said that the intimacy between them had ceased some nine to eleven months previously. Coulson said that the girl

Horrible and Bar-bari-ous Murder of Poor

JAEL DENNY,

A contemporary print of the murder of Jael Denny.

had been murdered, and that it was 'highly necessary' that Drory should go with him to the spot where the body lay. Drory agreed and he and the policemen rode in a cart towards Hammond's house then proceeded on foot to the meadow. As they neared the body however, Drory's composure deserted him. He slackened his pace and his unwilling legs could hardly carry him forward. As Coulson continued to the scene, Drory remained standing at a distance from the body, and appeared to cower away from it.

Coulson spent twenty minutes at the site. He knew Jael yet it was some time before he felt sure he recognised her. The girl's features were shockingly distorted, her face having been pressed so hard into the earth that her head was almost embedded in the ground and her nose was flattened to her face. Her hair was matted with blood and dirt and blood covered her face and clothes. The rope, which was about a yard long and slightly thinner than a little finger, was twisted three and half times around her neck and drawn so tight that it was embedded in the flesh and her neck was swollen above it. It was knotted towards the front of the neck. There were marks on her hands, showing that she had put up a considerable resistance. When the cord was unfastened, the flesh beneath was found to be cut and torn by the violence used. It was thought that the killer had approached her from behind and slipped a noose around her neck. When the examination was complete, a large field gate was brought and the body lifted onto it. As labourers transported the body to the Lasts' cottage, Coulson took Drory into custody. No mention had yet been made of Jael's pregnancy but as Coulson was supervising the carrying of the body into the cottage, Drory told Lenan that he had a letter at his house which would prove that the child

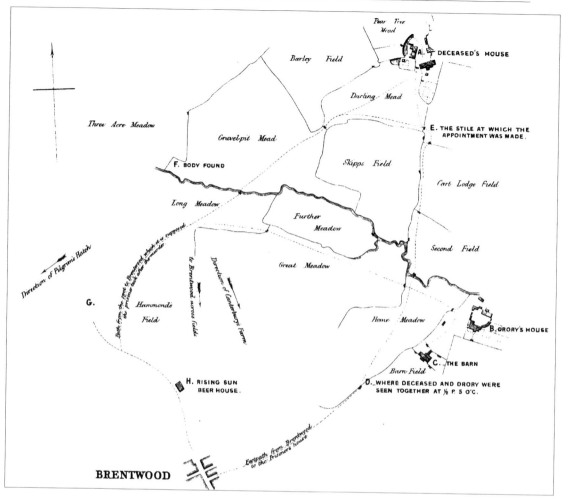

Contemporary map of Brentwood and the scene of the crime.

was not his. He added that fourteen days previously, Louisa had come to him and asked if his razors were all right. He had checked and returned to say that they were and asked why she had asked such a question, to which she answered that she had heard Jael say she would destroy herself and thought she would get at his razors.

Drory was taken indoors to be searched. Only money and keys were found in his pockets, but Coulson saw marks of what looked like fresh blood on his prisoner's breeches. Drory said that the marks were not blood but a preparation he had been giving to the calves, and he could show the police the pot it was kept in. Just before 9 p.m., Louisa Last arrived back at the cottage to be confronted by her worst possible fears.

The police accompanied Drory to his farm, where he pointed to a pot in an outhouse. There was a spoon in the pot and Coulson saw that both the pot and the spoon were covered in cobwebs and had obviously not been used for a long time.

The letter, written by Jael on 29 September, was in a box in Drory's bedroom, where the policemen also found some pieces of rope which looked very similar to the one used to strangle her.

That same afternoon, William Hammond's wife Elizabeth helped Louisa prepare her daughter's body for burial. When they removed the torn and stained clothing, they saw that the girl's chest was blackened with bruises. The left elbow was also bruised, and a patch of skin had been scraped away. Late on Sunday evening Drory, who was being held at Brentwood police station, was taken before Mr Lester, a county magistrate, and remanded for further questioning.

The post-mortem examination was carried out early on the morning of Monday 14 October by Mr John Williams, a surgeon of Brentwood. He found the 'eyes much distended with blood, pupils much dilated, and tongue protruding with swelling of face' and noted the laceration of the neck and severe bruising on the upper part of the chest. The congested state of the brain, heart and lungs were consistent with strangulation. The girl's right hand appeared to have been bitten, as there were the marks of teeth on the back. In the uterus was a healthy male foetus in the ninth month. Williams had no doubt that it was alive at the time of its mother's death.

The inquest was opened at 11 a.m. the same morning before Mr C.C. Lewis, the coroner for south Essex, at Hammond's farmhouse, which lay about midway between Drory's farm and Last's cottage. Captain McHardy, the Chief Constable of Essex, was present along with Police Superintendents May and Coulson. Drory's father attended

Brentwood police station.

having instructed Mr George Woodard, an attorney of Billericay, and the jury went to the Lasts' cottage to view the remains.

Louisa Last was shown Jael's crushed bonnet and torn cloak, and confirmed that they had not been damaged when her daughter set out. She denied having any conversation with Drory about his razors, and said that Jael had never threatened suicide.

The cord taken from Jael's neck and the cut piece of cord found at Drory's home were produced in court. Constable William Lenan said that the ends of the two pieces corresponded and they appeared to have formed one cord.

John Harris, a labourer employed by the Drorys, told the court that he had often seen Thomas and Jael together but about two or three months ago, he had heard Thomas say that he would like to 'shake her off' as he was carrying it on so far it would get him into trouble. Harris had witnessed the couple's afternoon meeting on 12 October, after which they had parted company and walked towards their own homes. After finishing his work, Harris overtook Jael on the footpath. 'Well, Jael, have you been for a walk?' he asked. 'Yes' she replied, 'I have been having a word or two with Mr Drory.' 'I saw you together at the top of the meadow,' said Harris, to which Jael said, 'Yes and I have to meet him again at half past 6 o' clock at the stile, at the bottom of the next meadow.'

William Stone Hubbard had seen Thomas go out at half past 6 or 7 p.m. on Saturday night, taking a basket of eggs with him, saying that he was going to Brentwood. Hubbard had gone to bed at 8 p.m. and was unable to say when Drory had returned home as he had his key with him. He next saw him at half past six on Sunday morning.

In view of Drory's claims that Jael had wanted to commit suicide, the coroner questioned John Williams closely. 'Can you tell us whether the deceased could have strangled herself in the manner and with the violence exhibited on the neck?' 'Certainly not,' replied Williams, adding that if she had attempted to strangle herself she would have been insensible before she caused so much violence to her neck. He also stated that the bruising was caused by someone kneeling on her chest shortly before death. The inquest was adjourned, and the stained clothing and the cobweb-encrusted pot were sent for analysis.

The crucial timing of events was discussed by the newspapers, aided as ever by local gossip and amateur sleuths. If Jael had been murdered at half past 6 then Drory if the perpetrator, must, it was reasoned, have moved very quickly as that evening, shortly after 8 o'clock, he was in Brentwood selling eggs to a carpenter called James Millington. Drory had next called at the Kings Head Inn, Brentwood, where, placing his empty basket on the bar, he ordered and ate six pennyworth of oysters and some bread and butter, then, together with the landlord Mr Parker, a butcher called Proud and a number of other tradesmen, he went into the public bar, drank two pints of 'half and half' (a blend of pale and dark beer) and smoked a pipe of tobacco and chatted amiably on farming matters. After Mr Proud and the others had left, Drory had a long conversation with Mr Parker (probably Samuel Parker, born about 1800) who had been to school with Thomas' father. The conversation touched on the changes that had taken place in the neighbourhood since Parker's childhood and he happened to mention the footpath near where the body of Jael Denny was later found, saying that he remembered it very well forty years ago. 'Had I known that Drory had committed this murder,' said Parker later, 'I could scarcely have spoken upon subjects more likely to call forth some emotion, but during the whole of this interview the prisoner's demeanour was perfectly calm and self possessed.'

Drory left the Kings Head shortly before 10 p.m., but his movements between then and 6 a.m. the following morning are unknown. A newspaper correspondent remarking that the body had been warm when found, pointed out that if the murder had been committed between 6 and 8 p.m. the previous night then it would have been exposed for upward of twelve hours to the bleak winds blowing from the Dengie Hundred and the Rochford marshes. This suggested that the murder could have occurred later, after 10 p.m. on Saturday.

In the interval between the inquest hearings, rumours flew around Doddinghurst. Drory, said to have been intending to publish the banns for his marriage to Miss Giblin on the following Sunday, was supposed to have predicted that Jael would not survive her confinement, or that she would kill herself as she did not know who the father of her child was. It was claimed that he had been seen sitting on a stile with a piece of cord, testing its strength, and had a spade and a pickaxe placed ready behind his door, with which to dig the grave of his victim. On 15 October, a report circulated that Drory had confessed, and this was widely believed, but the prisoner, who remained in custody at the police station, was still asserting his innocence.

On the Tuesday, Drory suddenly asked Constable Lenan how many turns of the rope were about Jael's neck. Lenan said he thought about three and a half, and Drory asked if they were very tight. 'They were tight enough to cause her death,' said Lenan. The prisoner asked him if he thought she could have done it herself. to which the policeman replied that he thought she could not. 'Well, I don't care,' said Drory, 'I didn't do it.'

On Thursday the 17th at 2 p.m., the adjourned inquest resumed at Brentwood police station, the prisoner being represented by Mr Hawkins of the home circuit and his solicitor. As Drory entered the court, he shook hands with his uncle and father but seemed less agitated than either of them. Jael's sister was also there, and at one point in the proceedings sobbed aloud and became hysterical. Other than that the inquiry was conducted 'in the midst of the most profound silence, and without any disturbing incident or any strong emotion being displayed.' When the evidence told most heavily against the accused, or the details seemed most likely to unnerve him, 'a deeper stillness seemed to spread over the audience, and every eye was directed to him.'

Drory showed the most extraordinary composure throughout. It was reported that 'his eye turned in an almost unembarrassed, though not careless manner, from point to point; his colour never changed, and his bearing under circumstances so trying, was unaffected and simple.' It was commonly thought at the time that character could be read in faces, but observers thought that any physiognomist who

Captain McHardy, Chief Constable of Essex. (Courtesy of the Essex Police Museum)

tried to see in Drory's face the 'ferocious traits' of someone who could carry out such a murder would have looked in vain. His youth and good looks, his face expressive only of mildness and innocence, created a very strong impression in his favour. Notwithstanding his 'smart active figure', many felt that he could hardly under normal circumstances have had the strength to overpower the taller, more strongly built Jael.

The most important witness was Dr Alfred Swaine Taylor, professor of chemistry and medical jurisprudence at Guy's Hospital, who had used a powerful magnifier to examine the stains on Drory's corduroy breeches. The stains were on the outside of the material and could not have come from the wearer. Some had been wetted in an attempt to wash them away, others had the hard, shiny appearance of clotted matter. Taylor concluded from the colour and the clotting that the stains were of blood, and the fact that it had clotted showed that it had flowed from a living person, or one recently dead. He added that great violence must have been used to cause an effusion of blood by strangulation, and he had never seen a case like it before.

Taylor also thought it was very possible that a woman advanced in pregnancy who had been killed at 6.30 p.m. might still be found warm at ten the next morning. Unfortunately, he had no means of judging how long the blood had been on Drory's clothing.

'Is there any difference,' asked a juryman, 'in the blood of an animal which a farmer is apt to get on his clothes, and that of a human being?' 'None whatever,' said Professor Taylor.

He said that he had only seen one case of someone strangling themselves, which had been done by putting a stick in a handkerchief and twisting it, and believed that it was not possible for someone to use such violence on herself as Jael had suffered as she would have lost consciousness before she could exert sufficient power.

Robert Moore told the court that Drory had not talked about Jael on the Sunday following the murder, but some time before, Moore had told him he thought he had committed himself with the girl, to which Drory had replied that he thought other young men had committed themselves with her as much as he.

The evidence having been completed, the coroner told the jury to dismiss from their minds any rumours they had read in the newspapers. The first point was whether the strangulation was homicidal or suicidal, and he believed the evidence was conclusive that Jael could not have strangled herself but had been killed by another person. It had been admitted that there had been an intimacy between the couple and she was close to her confinement, and wished to 'father the child upon him.' It would take seven or eight minutes to walk from the place of the meeting to where the body was found, and no more than that time to strangle her, and if it was then seven o' clock and Drory was seen in Brentwood at 8.10 p.m., there was ample time for him to get there.

The jury was absent for only fifteen minutes before they brought in a verdict of murder, naming Thomas Drory as the murderer. The prisoner was committed to the custody of Superintendent Coulson, by whom he was taken to Chelmsford Gaol by the next train.

The trial of Thomas Dory opened at Chelmsford on Friday, 7 March 1851 before Lord Chief Justice Campbell, and lasted two days. Outside, the Shire Hall resembled a besieged citadel and men with staves had to keep back the hundreds of spectators anxious to obtain admission. It was with some difficulty that the jurymen were able to enter the building and reach the jury box. There were only a few women in the crowds, 'it being understood that there would be evidence connected with the pregnancy of the deceased, which might possibly be not altogether consistent with their presence.'

The prosecution was conducted by Mr E.James QC and Mr Rodwell, while Drory was represented by Mr Clarkson, Mr Bodkin and Mr Hawkins. The respective solicitors were Mr James Parker of Chelmsford and Mr George Woodard.

Thomas Dory, looking calm and confident, pleaded not guilty in a firm voice. Some of the evidence was undoubtedly in his favour. With no way of determining the age of the blood on his breeches, any recent injury could have been the source. The court was told that at harvest time he had cut his little finger very badly and on going back to the farmhouse Louisa had dressed it for him, but it had taken a long time to heal. A piece of evidence given confidently on the first day of the inquest now appeared to have been mistaken. The police had been convinced that the rope around Jael's neck had been cut from the piece found in Drory's box, but on closer examination it was realised that the two pieces were of a different weave. Susan Twinn, who said that Jael's conduct was, as far as she had observed, 'becoming and proper,' said that Drory had called on her often, but revealed that another young man, whose name she did not know, had also visited Jael for about five weeks in January 1850.

Lord Chief Justice Campbell.

Other evidence did not favour the prisoner. Mr Williams, the surgeon, said that the first coil of the rope would have produced immediate insensibility and it would have been impossible for Jael to make the other two coils afterwards. He had examined Drory's mouth and thought that the bite marks on Jael's hand could have been inflicted by 'such a mouth as the prisoner's.'

Professor Taylor agreed with Williams that Jael could not have killed herself. He was questioned at length by Mr Bodkin, who made great efforts to prove that she could have done so, but was unshaken in his opinion.

Mr Clarkson addressed the jury, putting forward the best defence he could muster. He said that medical men had been known to make mistakes and pointed out that the police had been mistaken about the rope. Jael's letter, he claimed, was in the prisoner's favour, for if Thomas believed it would exonerate him from liability for the child then he had no motive to commit the crime. Clarkson said he would bring witnesses to show that there was considerable doubt on the question of whether or not the girl had committed suicide, and suggested that the prisoner should have the benefit of that doubt. He also promised to show that his client had an alibi for the time of Jael's death.

The defence's medical witnesses, none of whom had seen the body, were not convincing. A Mr Frederick Pollock, who said he felt there was some doubt in the case, admitted under questioning that his opinion would be influenced by surrounding circumstances; 'If I had found that the chest of the deceased was black, as if from a blow, or by strong pressure, that would have made a great difference,' he conceded. 'And the nose flattened to the face by the head being forced violently to the ground?' persisted Mr James. 'Yes,' admitted Pollock, 'that would have been a very strong circumstance to be taken into consideration.'

Susannah Hubbard said that on 12 October Drory had come home for his tea between 5 and 6 p.m. The meal would have taken about twenty minutes, after which he had to suckle the calves, which would also take about twenty minutes. He had then put some eggs in a basket and gone out at about half past 6 or 7. She had not seen him again until the next morning, when there was nothing unusual in his manner.

Isaac Day, a carter, had stopped at the Rising Sun beer shop about two miles from Brickhouse farm at about half past seven on 12 October and said that he had seen Thomas Drory near there. Jesse Bardell said he had also seen Drory near the Rising Sun at the same time, walking to Brentwood, but admitted that he had heard no clock strike and had not looked at any clock when he got home. The vagueness of these timings probably did not impress the jury.

The only witnesses who suggested that Jael may have been suicidal were George and Mary Wheal. George said he had heard her say that she carried a 'line' about with her in her pocket to make away with herself. Mary said that Jael had told her she had once tried to cut someone's throat, alluding, she thought, to Drory, and had tried to make away with herself using a line and a razor but something had always prevented her. Both said that they had thought at the time that Jael was not in earnest but 'gammoning' them. These stories were so melodramatic that the jury

Front page of a contemporary pamphlet.

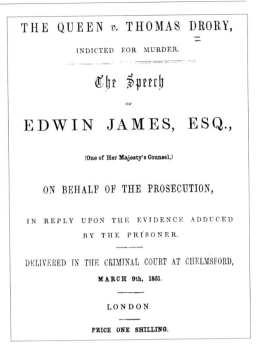

THE QUEEN *v.* THOMAS DRORY,

INDICTED FOR MURDER.

𝕿𝖍𝖊 𝕾𝖕𝖊𝖊𝖈𝖍

OF

EDWIN JAMES, ESQ.,

(One of Her Majesty's Counsel,)

ON BEHALF OF THE PROSECUTION,

IN REPLY UPON THE EVIDENCE ADDUCED
BY THE PRISONER.

DELIVERED IN THE CRIMINAL COURT AT CHELMSFORD,

MARCH 9th, 1851.

LONDON.

PRICE ONE SHILLING.

may well have concluded that the only 'gammoners' were Mr and Mrs Wheal. Five witnesses followed who knew Drory and his family and testified as to the good character of the prisoner, describing him as 'mild' and 'inoffensive'.

The jury deliberated for less than ten minutes, after which they found Thomas Drory guilty of the murder of Jael Denny. The Lord Chief Justice, in passing sentence of death, said that he entirely agreed with the verdict. Drory, who had been confident of an acquittal, did not appear to be moved. As the trial closed and people filed out of court it was found that someone had stolen both the rope with which the murder was committed and the plan of the spot where the crime had taken place. The tree growing near the murder site had already been stripped of its bark by curiosity hunters.

The condemned man's calm demeanour deserted him soon after his arrival at the gaol. He had to be helped to his cell by two warders, and there flung himself on his hammock and sobbed violently for almost an hour. He was later visited by the chaplain, Revd G.J. Hamilton, and the prison governor. Drory recovered enough to ask for the hammock to be replaced by an iron bedstead and his wishes were met, but despite this he remained restless and unable to sleep.

His friends and family called upon him often, but they did not discuss the crime. Mr Neale the governor, asked to describe the first visit of Drory's father on Monday, 10 March, said. 'They looked astounded at each other.' To which *The Times* comment was, 'Well they might.'

On the following day Drory had a long conversation with Neale, in which he admitted that he was the father of Jael's unborn child and that he alone had committed the murder. He said he had thought that because the deed was shrouded in darkness, it would be impossible for justice to reach him. Unfortunately, he could not resist attacking the character of the murdered girl by claiming that she had suggested the commission of other crimes, a statement which was not believed. Drory had been contemplating murdering Jael for some time and had a rope ready for the deed. After their first meeting on 12 October, he had gone home to get the rope from the farm. It had been assumed that he had bitten Jael's hand because both of his were engaged in holding the rope, but Drory stated that the marks were not teeth marks at all but from his fingernails.

COPY OF VERSES ON
DRORY AND JAEL DENNY.

AIR—"The Cruel Father and Affectionate Lovers."

E. HODGES, from Pitts Wholesale Toy Warehouse, 31, Dudley Street, Seven Dials.

WITHIN a dungeon I am bewailing,
  In grief and anguish I do complain,
My tender parents are sad lamenting,
  Borne down in sorrow, in care and pain.
I'm doomed to die on the fatal scaffold,
  My time is come and my glass is run,
Oh! God above look down in mercy,
  On Thomas Drory the Farmer's son.

I was brought up in famed Essex county,
  At Doddinghurst as you are aware,
When I seduced a pretty maiden,
  Named Jael Denny who loved me dear.
She was fair and handsome, a charming
    creature,
Kind and obliging, so free and young,
She little thought that she'd be murdered,
  By Thomas Drory the Farmer's son.

I first seduced her and then deceived her,
  I promised her she should be my wife,
And when I found she would be a mother,
  I resolved to take away the maiden's life.
I in a lane did appoint to meet her,
  And to the moment the maid did come,
There I betrayed her and cruel slayed her
  Oh, Thomas Drory the Farmer's son.

A rope I purchased to kill the maiden,
  And in a field I did throw her down,
I strangled her and I killed her infant,
  And left her laying upon the ground;

In the midst of health, in youth and bloom
  I slew the maid and from thence did run
Justice pursued me and apprehended
  Was Thomas Drory the Farmer's son.

Now I am tried and I am convicted,
  And doomed to die on the fatal tree,
The awful moments are fast approaching,
  Numbers are flocking my end to see.
That blooming maiden I have betray'd then
  The dreadful deed by me was done,
Night, noon, and morning, pray take a
    warning,
  By Thomas Drory the Farmer's son.

Adieu, my kind and my tender parents,
  I've brought upon you disgrace & shame,
Oh, pray forgive me since I acknowledge,
  My sentence just and I am to blame.
Jael Denny's blood loud does cry for ven-
    geance,
  The grave is open my time is come.
In health, in youth, in strength & vigour,
  Dies Thomas Drory the Farmer's son.

Oh, how could I basely slay that maiden,
  After that I had led her astray?
She often vowed she dearly loved me,
  And I in return took her life away.
I strove to hide that dreadful foul murder,
  And I from justice did strive to run,
While innocent blood did cry for vengeance
  On Thomas Drory the Farmer's son.

Contemporary verses about Drory and Jael Denny.

He had intended to make a formal written statement, but decided against it, and the magistrates, feeling that his admission of guilt was enough to satisfy justice and the public and considering also the feelings of his relatives, decided not to press him for further details.

In the aftermath of the trial rumours flew around the area. Miss Giblin was stated to have been staying in Chelmsford during the trial and to be 'in a condition that would render the matter doubly terrible to her and her friends.' Both rumours were, stated the *Chelmsford Chronicle,* utterly false.

There had been so many comments in the press about the incongruity of Drory's mild appearance and the cold savagery of his crime that the *Spectator* published an article on 'The Mildness of Murderers', which showed remarkable insight. 'Murder is not always ferocious in its aspect. The history of the affair indicates a shocking deficiency of feeling rather than positive malignancy an extreme coldness which could not comprehend strong feelings in others.' The leading trait in Drory's character was held to be 'intense selfishness.'

It was not until 23 March that Drory agreed to visit the prison chapel, but Revd Hamilton commented with regret that he 'seemed little able to comprehend the enormity of his crime.'

On 24 March Drory addressed a petition to the High Sheriff of the county of Essex in which he acknowledged that he was 'justly convicted.' After the usual pious comments hoping that his example might deter others from similar crimes, he asked the sheriff to order that the money found on him when searched by Superintendent Coulson – the sum of £8 11s 4d – might be given to Louisa Last 'as part restitution for the grievous injury' he had done her.

At 9 a.m. on 25 March, Drory was taken across the prison courtyard to the foot of the gateway tower, on top of which was the black scaffold. His body and limbs were trembling and he needed to be supported as he walked. At the foot of the staircase he was pinioned in a cell while the warders went to fetch Sarah Chesham, the Clavering poisoner who was to suffer on the same day. As soon as Drory appeared on the platform, faint and trembling with drooping head, the assembled crowd of 6 or 7,000 (some estimates suggested up to 15,000) were hushed into silence. Consisting mainly of smock-frocked labourers they had been assembling since 6 o'clock that morning from all parts of the surrounding countryside, some of whom had walked 12 to 15 miles to be there, and behaved in an orderly fashion apart from the shrill voices of boys at play and the cries of orange vendors. The newspapers observed that there were hardly any respectable people there 'but a most disgusting number of women', some of them dressed as if for a fair, with flowers in their bonnets.

The executioner was William Calcraft, whose victims suffered from his preference for the short drop and thus were slowly strangled to death. A white cap was placed over the prisoners' heads, the rope was adjusted, and the bolt was drawn. The death struggles of both were clearly visible – and being of light weight both 'died hard.' Thomas Drory was buried within the precincts of the gaol.

3

THE LOVE MATCH

Great Bromley, 1871

In 1871, the normally peaceful life of Backhouse Wenden, a farmer of Great Bromley, was disrupted by scandal and murder. Backhouse, born about 1822, was the owner of Manning Farm, also called Blue Gate farm, where he lived with his wife Mary Ann and two of their daughters, Annie, and Ellen Day Wenden, aged twenty. The family farmed 150 acres and employed nine men and four boys.

The Wendens, who did not regard themselves as socially far above their employees, associated freely with them, and were happy for them to call at the farmhouse. A frequent visitor was William Kittel (the name often appears as Kettle in census returns), who lived in a cottage about half a mile from the farmhouse. He had worked for Backhouse Wenden for many years and the two men were of similar age. (William may have been the 'William Kittle' baptised at Thorrington on 17 November 1822). In 1846, William had married labourer's daughter Elizabeth Head, who was about six years his junior, and by 1871 the couple had seven children, six of whom, aged between two and eighteen, still lived with their parents.

The Kittels' cottage was a wretchedly miserable home. William, described as 'a most unprepossessing-looking middle aged man', often accused his wife of being slothful. When asked how his parents got on together, their fourteen-year-old son Joseph said, 'They did not agree of a night.' He said that as soon as his father came home from his work, his parents would start to argue, William complaining that Elizabeth did not go out gleaning sooner in the morning. When William was out at work, Elizabeth was normally in good spirits, although she sometimes complained to Mrs Mary Ann Starling, a labourer's wife who lived a quarter of a mile away, that William did not give her enough money to provide for the family. Shortly before the 1871 harvest, Joseph saw William drag Elizabeth out of bed and threaten to throw her out of the window. This was so upsetting that the boy left home and thereafter slept in a barn.

On 5 October 1871, Elizabeth and some of her children had been picking sloes in a field belonging to Backhouse Wenden, and both she and the children had eaten some sloes. The family must have been hungry for sloes are very tart and are not normally eaten raw. Later, Elizabeth and her children all suffered from sickness and diarrhoea which they attributed to the sloes, but while the children recovered quickly Elizabeth's condition did not improve. Dr John Will Cook, a general practitioner of Manningtree, was asked to visit her on 8 October. Elizabeth lay in bed, in a filthy condition. She told Cook, who had never seen her before that she suffered from liver disease. Cook was there for only a few minutes and prescribed medicine for the stomach complaint.

Susannah Turner, wife of a labourer of Great Bromley, saw Elizabeth at 4 p.m. that afternoon and asked her how she was. 'Very ill indeed,' said Elizabeth unhappily, 'I can't tell you how I feel,' adding that she had been unable to keep any food down for three days. 'Poor creature,' said Susannah, 'how bad you are; does your husband know how ill you are?' 'He does not care,' said Elizabeth.

The sick woman was in need of nourishment, and kind-hearted Backhouse, hearing that the family was in financial distress, provided 4s so that a neighbour, Eliza Kittle (sometimes spelt Kettle), the wife of labourer Charles Kittle, who was no relation to William, could buy mutton chops to make her some broth. Eliza, who lived ten minutes walk away, visited Elizabeth between 4 and 5 p.m. and found her 'looking very bad.' She called again at 9 a.m. the next morning, finding Elizabeth still in bed and feeling much worse, and gave her some mutton broth. On the same day, Ellen Wenden, who was said to be 'of a cheerful kindly affectionate disposition,' went to the cottage taking some warm porridge in a basin. She also brought with her a packet of maize flour to make more porridge, which she left on the table.

When Eliza returned for another visit, William was at the house and she commented on the fact that his wife was wearing nothing but an old skirt. 'No old sow ever had to lay like this,' she said. He replied that he couldn't make out what his wife did with her things, 'he kept buying them and she kept selling them.'

Elizabeth's condition had by then so deteriorated that anyone who saw her believed that she could not live long, but the end still came sooner than expected.

Between 1 and 2 a.m. on the morning of 10 October, William Kittel went to Eliza and told her that his wife was dead and asked her to perform the usual offices for her. Eliza said she would but only if Mrs Starling also came. William went to see Mrs Starling, who agreed to come, and the two women went to the cottage. They found the corpse of Elizabeth Kittel lying on the bed, and in the bed were three children, eleven-year-old Maria, five-year-old Sarah and George, who was just two. The younger children were hugging their mother's body in great distress and had to be gently prised away. The body was naked, covered only with an old pair of trousers and an old skirt. The earthenware chamber pot was broken into several pieces, and there was a pool of dark clotted blood on the floor. There was vomit on the floor and the bed, and a wash tub in the room was half full of it. The source of most of the blood appeared to be a 3in long wound on Elizabeth's buttock, but there was also a large cut across her nose, an abrasion on her temple and other scratches on her body. William said that the chamber pot had broken while Elizabeth was sitting on it and this had caused the injury to her buttock, and she had then fallen against the bedstead and cut her nose. He had found her lying on the floor.

Mrs Starling and Eliza sent William to get some wood to make a fire so they could wash the body. Kittel said he had no chopper to chop wood but when the women removed the bedding from the bedstead they found a chopper lying underneath. They also found two beer bottles and a medicine bottle in the room. Dr Cook was called, and signed a death certificate stating that the cause of death was liver disease and exhaustion.

William Kittel was not without assistance for on the morning of Elizabeth's death, Ellen Wenden took charge of the cottage, washed the children and saw that the place was thoroughly cleaned. She even made the arrangements for Elizabeth's funeral.

The inquest on Elizabeth Kittel was held on 12 October. Dr Cook did not examine the body, but after hearing evidence of the fall and loss of blood, he changed his mind and gave the cause of death as 'syncope from loss of blood, the result of the wounds', syncope defined as 'abstraction of blood from the heart caused by the loss of blood.' He attributed the sickness and diarrhoea to the eating of sloes.

The inquest attributed death to natural causes, and Elizabeth was buried on 17 October. On 17 December, Ellen Wenden, described as 'rather good looking' with 'a frank, bright, and cheerful countenance', married the unprepossessing William Kittel at Tendring Register Office. The groom gave his age as thirty-nine but he was probably forty-nine years of age.

It was inevitable that William Kittel should have known Ellen Wenden for most if not all of her life, but it appeared that from a very early age the girl had formed a strong attachment to him. William often visited the farmhouse to see Ellen, although it is not known when their flirtation became an affair. Ellen was later to claim that her father knew all about the wedding, but it is notable that it did not take place until just after she had reached the age of twenty-one and no member of her family was a witness. If her parents disapproved there was nothing they could do, and they may have decided to make the best of things.

This unusual wedding excited considerable comment amongst the neighbours and was soon the talk of the village. Mrs Caroline Cracknell, the wife of a farmer of Great Bromley, knew the Wendens well and recalled that in April 1871 she had been at their house when Ellen had said to William, 'Go and get me a few sticks; bless your old heart!' This may have seemed overly familiar but worse was to follow. About a week to ten days afterwards, Mrs Cracknell was at the house again and saw Ellen and William sitting on a chair together (whether side by side or with Ellen on William's lap, she did not reveal). Mrs Wenden rebuked them and told William to go and do his work, but both went out into the passage. A few moments later there was a noise and she looked out into the passage and saw William and Ellen on the floor together. Mrs Wenden came in and reprimanded them and they went out. A little later Ellen came in and said, 'that's the man I want, and that's the man I'll have.' 'For shame, Ellen,' exclaimed Mrs Cracknell, 'He's a married man!' to which Ellen just laughed. Not long afterwards, Ellen was visiting Mrs Cracknell when her daughter, Emily, asked Ellen why she did not get married. Ellen replied that she would before long and she knew the one she would have.

Mrs Starling recalled that in the summer of 1871 Ellen used to talk about being married and had predicted that she would be married before Christmas and it would be to an 'old man.' On another occasion she had said that she would be married to the man she liked. That man was obviously William Kittel.

George Bloice, a labourer of Great Bromley, had also heard William say he liked Miss Ellen, and knew that as soon as he got home in the afternoon he almost always went to the Wendens to see her. That summer Ellen had been away for several weeks in Suffolk visiting a cousin, a farmer called Norman, to help out while his wife was ill. She returned shortly before the harvest, and soon afterwards, Bloice had seen Ellen and William in the cowshed, kissing.

Several women also remembered comments that Ellen had made which aroused grave suspicions about the death of Elizabeth Kittel. If nothing else they showed that Ellen had had considerable animosity towards the wife of the man she wanted.

Eliza Kittle remembered that on 9 October she had been on her way home and met Ellen, carrying a basin covered with a cloth, on her way to Elizabeth's house. Eliza said that the patient was 'very bad' and Ellen replied, 'It serves the old bitch right; nothing is too bad for her; but I am going to carry her something.' Later Ellen was walking back from the Kittels' house carrying a basin and spoon, when she met Mrs Starling and her neighbour Mrs Elizabeth Young. Asked how Mrs Kittel was, Ellen had said 'very ill', adding that she believed she would die. Later that day Ellen was at Mrs Starling's house and Mrs Young who had been visiting asked how Elizabeth was to which Ellen had replied that she did not know, adding 'the old bitch, I could throw her on the fire for two pins.' On the day after Elizabeth's death, Ellen had written to Mrs Cracknell, sending her some cloth and asking her to make mourning clothes for the family, saying, 'Poor man, she was a wretch indeed. She sold everything out of the house.' It wasn't the first time Ellen had arranged for clothes to be made for the Kittle children; she had done so in July 1871. On 17 October Ellen told Mrs Starling, 'I am glad the old bitch is dead; and if I had known it she should have been dead before.' Quite what 'it' was Mrs Starling didn't relate.

It also appeared that on 5 October Elizabeth Kittel had had more than sloes to upset her. Ellen had brought her and her children some beer in a bottle, and Elizabeth and the children had vomited after drinking it. She had then brought them another bottle of beer and they had again been sick. That day, Ellen had been accompanied by two or three girls, who were her cousins, and they had drunk some of the beer but were not sick. Some of the witnesses to this event said Elizabeth did not drink any beer, but others thought that she had drunk from the bottle, or at least saw her putting it to her mouth. Charles Kittle believed that Ellen had had some beer and thought he had seen her being sick in the field.

The villagers talked about their suspicions and inevitably they discussed the things they recalled Ellen saying, and compared notes. Although they could only remember one occasion on which Ellen had visited the sick woman, it was rumoured that Ellen had been back and forth to the cottage during the whole course of Elizabeth's illness, sometimes going twice a day, and taking her things to eat and drink. Someone also recalled that at the inquest on Elizabeth, Backhouse Wenden had been foreman of the jury.

Ellen's help in caring for Elizabeth and cleaning the Kittel cottage after her death now had a sinister look, especially considering the speed with which she had taken over. On the morning of Elizabeth's death Mrs Starling had stayed in the Kittels' cottage until 7, then she had gone to the Wendens' house and, seeing Ellen, told her that Elizabeth had died and asked for some clothes to put on the corpse. Mrs Starling said she had asked William Kittel to wake them up and tell them his wife was dead, but he had not done so. 'He could very easily have woke me,' Ellen replied, 'as I knew she would die to-night.' Mrs Starling got the clothes and went back to the Kittels' cottage. Soon afterwards Ellen arrived. She asked for the two beer bottles, saying they were the ones she had sent the beer in, and took them away. She also asked that the bed and bedding be burnt and asked Mrs Starling to scrub the house. Thereafter Ellen came to the house every day, gave orders as to what was to be done there, and arranged the funeral, saying that William had told her she might do as she pleased.

On 3 April 1872, the body of Elizabeth Kittel was exhumed, and Dr Cook and a Mr Nunn of Colchester carried out a post-mortem. The viscera were found to be 'wonderfully preserved' and coated in places with a film of bright yellow, both of which suggested the presence of poison. Samples were taken and sent to Dr Stevenson, lecturer in chemistry at Guy's Hospital. In the stomach he discovered large white gritty grains, which tests showed were chiefly composed of white arsenic. The yellow substance was a mixture of white arsenic and yellow sulphide of arsenic, which was often produced from the white arsenic after death thorough putrefaction. Altogether he extracted five grains of arsenic from the stomach alone, and there was more arsenic in the other viscera. Some of the arsenic he was sure had been administered in the 24 hours prior to death. The fatal dose for an adult was two grains.

No member of the Kittel family had had access to arsenic, but enquiries soon revealed that Ellen had. When Ellen had gone to stay with Mr Norman, her mother had asked her to obtain from him a supply of poison for killing mice. When Norman drove Ellen home he brought the poison, which he had obtained from a veterinary surgeon, and gave it to Ellen's parents. The poison was arsenic and it was mixed with verdigris, a preparation of copper sometimes used as a fungicide, and hog's fat. It was a preparation commonly used by farmers as a dressing for sheep. The bottle was recovered by the police and given to Dr Stevenson for analysis. Norman had other packages of poison which he kept locked away in a chest, and these too he gave to the police.

Mrs Starling saw Ellen after the body was exhumed and said 'what a talk' there was about it. She wished there had been no inquest, for if there had not been one, she believed the body would have been 'taken up' before. Ellen said she was glad there had been an inquest and asked what people were saying Elizabeth had died of. Mrs Starling replied that some said 'cold' and some said 'fever' but a great many said she was poisoned. 'I did not poison her,' said Ellen. 'I did not want to get rid of her so bad.' Astonished, Mrs Starling asked, 'Then you wanted to get rid of her a little?' Ellen made no reply.

Eliza Chilver, the wife of a labourer, had also talked to Ellen about the exhumation and Ellen had said she wondered how the news had got out that her family had poison, as only her father, mother, sister Annie and herself knew about it, and they had had it for two years. Eliza said she need not wonder as she herself had told Mrs Charles Kittle. Ellen asked Mrs Chilver whether she thought that if someone was sick, this would bring the poison up, supposing that it had been taken.

William too had had poison on his mind. He asked Elizabeth Young's husband, James, whether if anyone was poisoned and a doctor went to see them he would know what was the matter with them. William had explained his interest by telling James a story which had recently been bandied about the village, concerning a man and his wife who couldn't agree. The man had cooked a pudding for his wife and poisoned it, but she had not eaten it because a spider dropped into it. The man had later eaten the pudding by mistake, and died, but not before confessing his guilt.

On 5 April, Ellen and her husband were arrested on suspicion of murder. William said, 'I did not do it' and Ellen, whose talent for careless comments was unabated, said, 'oh, they say she was poisoned then, but it will take them all their time to prove it.' On the way to gaol Ellen coolly said to her husband, 'You know where you are, and I know where I am. You know nothing about it; I don't know what you do and you don't know what I do.' William's reply, if any, was unrecorded. Whatever the meaning underlying the words, they show that Ellen was the dominant partner in the marriage, the one who took charge of any situation and determined how it was to be dealt with. They were remanded on the following day, and Ellen said to William, 'If we are guilty we shall have to suffer, but it will take them all their time to prove it.'

The enquiry, which was held before a special sitting of the Mistley magistrates, took three days. The *Essex Standard* commented: 'She is an ordinary-looking country girl, and her infatuation for Kittel (who, in addition to being so much her senior, has by no means an attractive exterior) can hardly be understood. Beyond paying attention to the evidence, they displayed the greatest nonchalance.'

During the course of the hearing a great deal was made of the hidden chopper, hinting that this and not the chamber pot might have been the cause of Elizabeth's injuries, however this theory was exploded when Maria Kittel gave evidence. On the night of Elizabeth's death she had been sleeping in the same bed as her mother. She had been woken by William asking where her mother was and found her lying on the floor by the side of the bed. There was a piece of broken chamber pot sticking in her and she pulled it out.

William's eldest daughter Elizabeth, who was in service, said she had visited the family in June 1871 and her father had said that he wished her mother was dead and 'it would be a good job if she was.' He had been arguing with his wife before he

Mistley police station.(Courtesy of the Essex Police Museum)

and his daughter went out and had said that if she didn't get out of his way he would kick her out. Elizabeth said that her father had been complaining about the children looking untidy, but had never said that his wife had got rid of things from the house.

On 18 April William Kittel was discharged, but Ellen was committed for trial at the next assizes. Mr Pearce, the barrister who defended her, asked for her to be granted bail on the grounds that she was pregnant, and did not want the disgrace of giving birth to a child in prison. The application was refused and Ellen 'who appeared to treat the matter with the utmost indifference' was taken to Chelmsford Gaol. Just before this decision was given, Ellen started to say, 'I did not burn the paper' but was quickly silenced. Henry Jones, solicitor for the prosecution, asked that the words 'I did not burn the paper' be added to the statement she had signed as to reserving her defence. He was telling the court that he did not know to which paper her words referred, when Ellen again butted in, saying, 'What got the poison in.' Henry Goody solicitor for the defence, quickly advised Ellen not to say anything at all. It later emerged that it had been rumoured that there was another source of poison in a paper, which Ellen had burnt.

With Ellen in custody, William went about his work as usual but on 2 May he was delivering a wagon load of corn to Mistley when a large crowd assembled and he was pelted with stones, brickbats, bags of flour, offal and rotten eggs. The hubbub was such that the police were sent for. Later that morning, at Colchester, a crowd of women and children gathered and threatened him with violence. The police had to hustle him away through some back gardens, then took him over the railway and through some meadows into Greenstead Road.

The trial opened on 15 July 1872, when Ellen, who had then been married for seven months, appeared in the dock very heavily pregnant and pleaded 'not guilty' in a firm clear tone of voice. A chair was placed in the dock for her. The prosecutors were the Hon George Denman QC and Mr Croome, while Mr Serjeant Parry and Mr Pearce conducted the defence. Ellen, said the prosecution, 'had the strongest motive a woman could have' to get rid of the wife in order to succeed her.

'It was,' said Mr Denman, with the voice of long experience, 'one of the mysteries of crime, how persons who cherished murderous designs against others and had every desire to conceal their intentions and feign kindness for their intended victims, should nevertheless, be unable at times to resist the impulse to disburden their minds of the feelings of hatred which really actuated them.'

Dr Cook was called to give evidence and despite everything his opinion of the cause of death was unchanged from the one he had given at the inquest. Dr Stevenson had compared the grains of arsenic found in Elizabeth's stomach with those found in the mixture sent to Ellen's father. They corresponded well but he could not go so far as to say they were the same. The arsenic in the stomach however had been free of copper, a constituent of verdigris, and this did not support the assumption that it came from the mixture.

That afternoon, Ellen Wenden went into labour, but she remained in the dock. A couch was brought for her to lie on, and she was attended by doctors. She continued in labour as the trial progressed and at the end of the day Mr Serjeant Parry said he would not call any witnesses. The hearing was adjourned at half past five with Ellen having been in pain for two or three hours. Despite the obvious indications, the court was told that it was thought that she would be better after a rest and the trial could continue the next day. At a quarter past nine that evening Ellen gave birth to a healthy full-term son in Chelmsford Gaol. The following morning it was agreed that it was impossible to continue with the trial. The jury was discharged, and it was ruled that Ellen would be tried again at the next assizes.

Ellen's second trial commenced at Chelmsford Assizes on 24 October 1872, before Mr Baron Martin. The prosecution was led by Mr C. Pollock and Mr Croome, and Mr Serjeant Parry and Mr Pearce appeared for the defence. Ellen's parents and sisters attended, and showed throughout considerably more emotion than the prisoner, who, 'whether from consciousness of innocence or from strength of nerve, never showed the least anxiety, but sat or stood in the dock, calmly, though closely watching the evidence against her without a trace of uneasiness.' Ellen's self-control was so striking that sometimes, it distracted the attention of her relatives from the case itself.'

One of William's daughters told the court of being given the beer by Ellen, though she said it had tasted just as beer always did. Mrs Starling said that she had seen two of the children the day afterwards and their faces were swollen and 'their eyes looked bad.' A labourer who had been in an adjoining field said that

Ellen had been with the family for about an hour and he thought Ellen was also vomiting.

The neighbours who had previously given evidence about their suspicions, Mrs Starling, Eliza Kittle and Mrs Young, were all obliged to admit that they had said nothing until the police were making enquiries, and that they had discussed the matter with each other before giving evidence. It was also admitted that when Ellen visited the sick woman she had carried the basin and spoon quite openly, with no attempt made at concealment. Eliza was obliged to agree in cross-examination that her own daughter, after seeing Elizabeth Kittle, said that she thought she would die. As regarding the burning of the bed, the court was told that it had been in a very filthy state.

Dr Cook was asked pointedly whether the fact that arsenic had been found in the body altered his opinion as to the cause of death. He hesitated so long that the question was asked a second time. After another pause he said that he was still of the opinion that the immediate cause of death was loss of blood. Dr Stevenson, however, stated that he believed that loss of blood was not the sole cause of death because the blood vessels in the intestines were well filled.

The prosecution hoped to ask Dr Stevenson about the packages of poison the police had recovered from Mr Norman, but Serjeant Parry objected on the grounds that the packages could not be traced to the prisoner. There was some conference between counsel, after which Mr Pollock was obliged to concede that he could not trace possession of the packages to the prisoner, and the judge ruled that evidence about them was not admissible. Stevenson was only therefore questioned about the bottle known to have been in the Wenden house. He said he could not find any particles of arsenic in the bottle as large as the largest of those he recovered from the stomach. The judge observed that, 'he did not think the prosecution could make anything of this part of the case'. Dr Stevenson said that all he could state was that the particles in the stomach 'might' have come from the bottle. 'Or they might not, that is all' said the judge.

Dr Stevenson further testified that he had found 'slight traces' of copper in the viscera, but this could have come from 'various articles of diet.' He was reminded of the statement in his original report that the fact that the arsenic in the stomach had no trace of copper 'does not tend to support the hypothesis that the arsenic had been mixed with verdigris.' Arsenic had little taste, but verdigris was 'very nauseous and nasty.' Since the poisons in the bottle were mixed with grease, he was asked whether the effect of such a mixture in food would not be 'dreadfully nauseous and disgusting in taste.' 'It certainly would,' Stevenson replied. Was it possible, he was asked, 'to mix such a filthy stuff with food, such as gruel, without it being betrayed to the taste?' Stevenson said that it would 'be difficult to conceive of its being taken in food without its being at once rejected.'

The case for the prosecution closed and the court was adjourned to the following day, when the defence called no witnesses. Mr Pollock told the jury that 'there was the strongest possible evidence to show, not only that arsenic was there in her body, but they had evidence to show that the prisoner might, and very probably did, administer it,' adding, '... when a woman once lost her right feeling in matters of

The Shire Hall in Chelmsford.

this kind, she became worse than the most evil of men.' Mr Serjeant Parry emphasised that the question before the jury was not whether the prisoner could have
committed the act but whether it could be clearly proved that she did. The greater
part of the case against her was 'really only conjectural.' Regarding the relations
between Ellen and her husband, he cleverly portrayed Ellen as a simple, innocent
and easily led girl who had fallen under the spell of an experienced older man:

> He could not account for her conduct except on the ground of some infatuation. But
> how did they know that the poor girl had not been entangled by this man of mature
> age...and what arts might have been employed to seduce her?...Perhaps if they knew all
> the circumstances she might appear rather as an object of sympathy...

The 'monstrous theory of the prosecution', that she might have designed to poison
the wife in order to marry the husband, 'was suggested merely upon the strength of
a few idle and heedless expressions such as might have been dropped inconsiderately
by a foolish girl.' Despite rumours to the contrary, no evidence had ever been brought
to show that Ellen had attended Elizabeth from the 5 to 9 October, during which the
condition of the deceased had grown steadily worse. Even when Ellen did take food,
there could have been no poison in it or Elizabeth would have refused to eat it.

In Mr Baron Martin's summing up, he said that the case turned upon two points,
whether the deceased had died from arsenic and whether the prisoner administered
it. On the first point they needed to be satisfied that the poison was administered
with the intention of causing death and that it materially contributed to the death.
Regarding Ellen's actions, she had undoubtedly 'brought all her suffering on herself
by her own conduct' and 'roused a very strong feeling against her in the neighbourhood', however the suggestion that there was poison in the beer was 'all surmise'
and the attempt of the prosecution to prove that the arsenic found in the body was
the same as the arsenic to which she had access 'utterly and totally failed.' The girl's
conduct, he said, 'may have been reprehensible and may have laid her open justly

and naturally to suspicion' but the jury must direct their minds to what had actually been proved against her.

The jury did not even trouble to leave the box. They conferred together for a minute or two, and then returned a verdict of not guilty. This verdict, pointed out *The Times*, had been anticipated by everyone watching the case 'but it was not received with any expression of satisfaction.'

Ellen's self-control had hardly wavered throughout the trial. When she heard the verdict she flushed, rose up, curtseyed, thanked the jury, and then, 'as if suddenly remembering the severe comment made upon her conduct', flushed more deeply and sank down upon her seat, and was for a few moments overcome with emotion.

The crowds of people in the court waited for the family to leave, but the police, anticipating a demonstration, cleared the court and then took Ellen out by a secret passage. She was taken to Chelmsford Gaol to collect her child and returned home.

Ellen and William were fortunate to be cleared of Elizabeth's murder. It seems probable from Ellen's unguarded comments that she had had access to a source of pure arsenic, maybe the one she mentioned to Mrs Chilver as having been in the family's possession for two years. William's unwise questions of James Young strongly suggest that he may have been an accessory to his wife's murder, or at the very least suspected Ellen of it.

The Times, while agreeing with the jury's verdict, pointed out that there was still an unexplained mystery: 'Five grains of arsenic do not find their way into a sick woman's stomach without someone having administered them.' About the relationship between Ellen and William there could be no doubt. Their conduct was 'a painful exhibition of the deformity of which human passion is capable.' Not only that but their relationship appeared to have been unaffected by the trial. 'Such grossness is, we trust, exceptional, but that such a transaction should be possible in a metropolitan county affords matter for melancholy reflection.'

It is not known to what extent Backhouse and Mary Ann Wenden were affected by the scandal of their daughter's murder trial. As for Ellen and William, it would not have been surprising if the stress of the trial, the general censure of society, disapproval of the Wendens, ill-feeling in the neighbourhood and the almost thirty-year age difference would have quickly doomed their marriage. But Ellen's passion for her 'old man' was not an infatuation or some passing fad. Braving out all the comments and ignoring all obstacles, they stayed together, and raised ten children. Perhaps, despite all appearances, it was a genuine love match.

On 22 February 1893, Backhouse Wenden committed suicide. He had been depressed about the farming business, and had complained of his wife's drunkenness, which had caused him a lot of distress. His grandson, seventeen-year-old Alphonso Kittel, who worked as a labourer on Blue Gate farm, found him hanging from a beam in his barn. Ellen and William were only to be parted by his death in 1909, at the age of eighty-six. Ellen died in 1927, aged seventy-eight.

4

TWICE VEXED

Purleigh 1893

The agricultural village of Purleigh lies to the west of the Dengie peninsula, about three miles south of Maldon. In the 1890s the population numbered less than 1,000, and many inhabitants would have relied for employment on Hazeleigh Hall Farm, which lay about a mile to the north. The farm was occupied by Edward Arthur Fitch, who lived at Brick House on the Maldon road.

On the morning of Sunday, 16 April 1893, Joseph Moss, the son of Fitch's bailiff, noticed some sacks of corn lying on a bank by a field known as 'Pound Field'. He thought they were from a stack which had been stored in the barn, as there was no-one in the neighbourhood with similar sacks. He went to check the barn, but couldn't get in as the lock had been tampered with. Suspecting that there had been a robbery he informed his employer, who went to investigate. Moss went to Maldon and reported the robbery to Inspector Charles Edwin Pryke, and they went to the scene together, arriving at about 3 p.m.

Meanwhile, a far grimmer crime had been discovered. Herbert Patten, a carpenter of Purleigh, was walking with his sweetheart near Hazeleigh Hall, not far from the Queen's Head beer-house on the Chelmsford road, when he saw a patch of blood near the brow of a ditch close to Bellrope Gate. The ground had been trampled, suggesting that a violent struggle had taken place on the spot. Patten peered into the ditch, which was about 5ft deep, and to his horror he saw the body of a man. He would undoubtedly have recognised Sergeant Adam John Eves of the Essex Constabulary, who was in full uniform. Patten at once reported his find, and fetched Constable Chaplin of Stow Maries to the scene. Inspector Pryke, who was nearby investigating the robbery, was also alerted.

It was immediately obvious that the robbery and the murder were connected, for three sacks of grain were found about 9ft from the ditch. Eves, it was thought, had met with a gang of thieves carrying sacks of stolen corn from the barn late on Saturday night. The sergeant, who was described as 'an energetic young

Sergeant Eves, his cottage, the finding of the body, the Purleigh Bell and the Ramseys.

Sergeant Eves. (Courtesy of the Essex Police Museum)

police officer', must have challenged the thieves, who murdered him to avoid arrest. He had first been stunned by blows on the head and then his throat was cut with a knife. Two blood-smeared bludgeons were found by the side of the body and also a black hawthorn stick which belonged to Eves. He had had no time to defend himself for his truncheon was still in his pocket. The murderers had then abandoned the grain, and the quantity found suggested to the police that the thieves had provided themselves with a horse and cart in which they had made their escape.

Adam John Eves was born in Hutton near Billericay in 1857, the son of a wheelwright. In 1871, fourteen-year-old Adam was working as a gardener, but in March 1877 he joined the Essex police force. He married Elizabeth Ann Ettritch in Rochford in 1878, and the couple had no children.

After serving at several stations in Essex – he was at Aldham in 1881 – he arrived in Purleigh in January 1891. Eves was considered by his colleagues and the public to be a capable and efficient officer. He had on several occasions been complimented by the Chief Constable and by the court of quarter sessions for the intelligent way he had detected crimes. He was also a member of the St John Ambulance association and more than once had been praised for his skill when attending accidents. He was promoted to acting sergeant in February 1893.

Eves had left home at 8.45 p.m. on 15 April. He had last been seen at about 10 o'clock that night leaving the Oak Inn, Hazeleigh, where he had given the landlord a reward notice about the poisoning of rooks in the neighbourhood. On his way home he would have passed Hazeleigh Hall Farm, walked along the top of Pound Field, past Bellrope Field and along Bellrope Lane. He would normally have returned home at about 6 a.m. on Sunday morning, but his wife had not been alarmed, imagining that he had been detained by a fire in the neighbourhood or some other duty.

On the discovery of Eves' body, Superintendent Halsey of Latchingdon was sent for and he telegraphed Captain Edward McLean Showers, the Chief Constable of Essex who was stationed at Chelmsford, and Deputy Chief Constable Mr Raglan Somerset. The scene of the murder was searched and Constable Chaplin found three more sacks of grain in a nearby pond. Pryke arranged for the body to be lifted from the ditch. Eves had been dead for some hours and his body was stiff and cold. It was taken by cart to Eves' home, a cottage on the Chelmsford road.

Dr George Melnoth Scott, who practised at Maldon, was sent for and saw the body of Sergeant Eves lying on the floor of a room in the officer's house. It was dressed in full uniform including the overcoat. He examined the body and found that all the injuries were on the head and throat. There were three wounds on the forehead, one over the left eyebrow running upwards and outwards. On the neck and throat there were three cuts, two being under the left ear. All the wounds had been inflicted during life. The head injuries were not enough to cause death, which had resulted from haemorrhage from the large wounds in the throat.

Richard Davis.

Meanwhile, the police were following a trail of scattered wheat which led towards Bellrope Field. Against the first gate and under Bellrope Gate were more trails of wheat and near a gap in the hedge was a sack and two pea bags containing wheat. The sack had a distinctive marking, being branded 'Ingledew and Devonport Brothers' Market, 1892, I. and D.'

The wheat trail led in the direction of the houses of brothers John and Richard Davis, who at once became suspects for both the robbery and murder. John William Davis was born in 1855 and his brother in 1862. Both were agricultural labourers. John was married with a son, but Richard, who was unmarried, lived with his parents, Richard Snr and Elizabeth. The distance from Hazeleigh Hall to Richard Davis' home was half a mile. From the Davis' cottages to where the body was found was about a third of a mile. Eves and the Davises would have encountered each other often, as their cottages were all in the same one-mile radius, and there had been earlier conflict between the policeman and the family. In 1891 Eves, suspecting John Davis of poaching, had tried to search him and a lengthy struggle had ensued, during which the powerful thickset Davis had aimed a blow at Eves with a gun barrel. Eves had drawn his truncheon and knocked him down. As a result, Davis had been fined for poaching and sentenced to two months hard labour for the assault. Eves had also given evidence in court against John and Richard's brother, Charles, who was charged with being drunk and disorderly. Richard had no criminal convictions but was suspected of receiving stolen property.

On 15 April the Davis brothers had been at work at Hazeleigh Hall Farm, threshing wheat. The wheat had been fed into the machine by labourer Thomas Choat and the machine was operated by thirty-nine-year-old James Ramsay. The Davises had given the tallies to Ramsey, who made a return of 14 quarters (a quarter being one fourth of a hundredweight or 28lbs) as threshed. During that day's threshing the wheat had accidentally been mixed with barley. The grain had been stored in pea-sacks.

Accompanied by Superintendent Halsey and several police officers, Pryke went to John Davis' house. He knocked at the front door and, receiving no reply, went round the back. Finding the door unfastened the police entered and searched the house, but found no grain. They then went to Richard Davis' home, where they saw Richard Davis, and his parents.

Pryke told them that some grain had been stolen and that Sergeant Eves was murdered. Mr and Mrs Davis said 'It is a bad job' but Richard, who was looking pale and very agitated, made no reply. Pryke told Richard that he was suspected of being involved in the crime, and the Davises gave the police permission to search the premises. In a room at the far end of the house Pryke found three sacks containing wheat and barley. Pryke went upstairs and found another sack full of barley and in the next bedroom there were three more sacks of barley and one of flour. A spade with a bloodstained handle was found at the house. Richard Snr said the grain was his – he had grown it in his own field two years ago. After questioning Richard, Pryke saw his brother John outside and questioned him too.

Pryke examined John Davis' clothes and found bloodstains on the waistcoat and trousers. There were bloodstains on the back of Richard's jacket which looked as if they had been recently scraped. His boots had been oiled but also seemed to be stained with blood. Both brothers carried knives, which were confiscated.

The police did not have far to look for the cart, which they felt sure had been used by the thieves. A bloodstained cart was found in a shed at the back of the Davis' house. The Davises said the blood was from a sheep's head and that the cart had not been used for several days, however a recent wheel track led from John Davis' house across a field and in the direction of the ditch in which the body was found. Several bloodstained sacks with markings, which suggested they had been amongst those stolen, were found in a pond in front of Richard Davis' house. They had been rolled around brickbats and sunk.

Richard Davis' parents were not suspected of having taken part in the crime. Richard Jnr, it was established, slept downstairs in the house and his parents upstairs, so he could easily have slipped out at night without disturbing them.

Maldon police station. (Courtesy of the Essex Police Museum)

Edward Fitch examined the sacks and grain found in the Davises' house, but was unable to positively identify them as his property. The sacks were, however, branded similarly to those found by the body. Fitch also knew that Davis Snr's claim to ownership of the grain could not be true as the field in question had been uncultivated for at least four years. In his opinion the grain had been grown in 1892.

As the investigation continued the number of suspects increased. It was found that the tally of threshed wheat submitted by James Ramsey was wrong, and it was believed that he had deliberately falsified the account to conceal the planned theft.

On the Sunday night the police learned that James Ramsey had been seen near John Davis' house on Saturday night talking to Charles Sales, the Davises' brother -in-law. A year earlier, Eves had told Pryke that he suspected Sales of receiving stolen grain. Suspecting that Sales and Ramsey had been plotting the robbery, Pryke went to Sales' house and asked him where he had been on Saturday night. Sales looked agitated, and said that he was home early that night and had not seen either of the Davises. He claimed he had only heard about the murder an hour before. The police also searched the house of Charles Davis, but found nothing incriminating.

Early on the Monday morning, Pryke and another officer rode to Purleigh in the county cart and arrested Sales. Noticing bloodstains on his waistcoat, Pryke asked him to account for them. Sales said, 'It is blood; it is from a meat bone I bought.' When he removed his jacket Pryke saw bloodstains on the back of the waistcoat. Pryke then charged him with the murder. A search of Sales' house revealed pea sacks, which were marked in a similar way to those found in the Davises' pond.

The barn from which corn was stolen. In front are the witness, Choat, and the policemen who arrested Ramsey.

James Ramsey Jnr.

Sales denied any involvement in the crimes, saying that he looked upon Eves as a friend. In the previous April he had injured his ankle and Eves had bandaged it.

Pryke handed four samples of the grain found in the Davises' house to a miller and farmer Henry Charles Cocks of Heybridge. Cocks reported that in his opinion it had been grown in three different fields in 1892, and any statement in which it was claimed that it had been grown in one field two years ago was false.

Another man, thirty-seven-year old local labourer John Bateman, who often slept out in the fields, also fell under suspicion and was arrested. Bateman said he had 'laid rough' on both Saturday and Sunday night and that stains found on his clothes were of spilt porter.

On the morning of Monday 17 April, John Davis, Richard Davis Jnr, Charles Sales and John Bateman were charged with the murder of Sergeant Eves. That evening they were taken before the county justices at Maldon. All four were remanded for a week.

It was labourer Thomas Choat who supplied the evidence needed to arrest James Ramsey. Choat told the police that Ramsey had used threatening language against Eves on several occasions, saying, 'If ever I meet him I should not give him a chance. I should give him the first blow.' Ramsey, he added, said that he always carried something in his cart for that purpose. Choat said that he had seen Ramsey talking to John Davis on the Friday morning and they seemed to be planning something.

On 18 April, Sgt Joseph William Hurrell and PC Chaplin went to Mr Lloyd's mill at Hazeleigh at 12.30 p.m. and found Ramsey at work in the blacksmith's shop. He was asked if he would accompany them to the Queen's Head to see Superintendant Halsey, 'as we have received information of statements and threatening language you have used towards the deceased man Eves.'

Ramsey denied that he had ever threatened Eves. When asked where the trousers were that he was wearing on Saturday, he insisted that they were the ones he currently wore. Thomas Choat was brought in and said that the trousers Ramsey was wearing were not the ones he had worn on Saturday.

Hurrell and PC Harrington went to Ramsey's cottage and found eleven pea bags and a sack under Ramsey's bed, similar to the ones in which stolen grain was found. Traces of blood were found on Ramsey's clothing. Ramsey claimed that on the Saturday night he and his son, fifteen-year-old James Jnr, were at Maldon. They had got home at 9 p.m. and didn't go out again.

James Jnr now became a suspect, especially when the police were told he owned a gun and a knife. At 1 p.m., Constables Jellis and Chaplin found James Ramsey Jnr at work in a field at New Hall Farm Purleigh. He handed over his knife and, contrary to what his father had said, told the police that he had been at the White Hart, Hazeleigh at 10 p.m. on Saturday, fetching beer for his mother. Jellis looked at the boy's clothes and saw blood spots on his trousers. 'If you find any blood that ain't his as I cut my finger on Friday,' said James.

'How do you know I was looking for blood?' said Jellis. 'I never told you so.' Jellis arrested the boy, and on the way to Purleigh asked him if he had a licence for his revolver. Young Ramsey said it was not a revolver it was a pistol and he didn't have a licence as he hadn't carried it. 'You must have carried it or people would not have seen it,' said Jellis, stating that he knew Ramsey had shown it to people. Ramsey was obliged to admit that he had shown it to one or two people but protested that he had not fired it.

On the same day Dr Scott carried out the post-mortem. The top of Eves' skull was cracked from the left side of the crown, and there was bruising of the brain. The gash in the throat had cut the main vessels of the left side of the neck, and had gone so deep that the point of the knife had marked the vertebrae.

On 22 April Adam John Eves was buried at Purleigh churchyard, and the funeral drew a large gathering of the county constabulary and the public.

Meanwhile the local newspapers had been making enquiries and picking up all the gossip about the suspects. On 22 April the *Essex Standard* stated that the Davis brothers, Bateman and Sales, 'bear bad characters in the district, and are known as idlers and poachers.' Bateman, it was claimed, had a wife who he didn't support and who had turned him out of the house. He spent winter in the workhouse and in warmer weather slept rough in the fields. Sales, said to be forty-seven, was 'a good-for-nothing rascal. He came to Purleigh from Forest Hill, Sydenham, S.W. two or three years ago, having married the sister of the prisoners Davis. He has two daughters.' It was

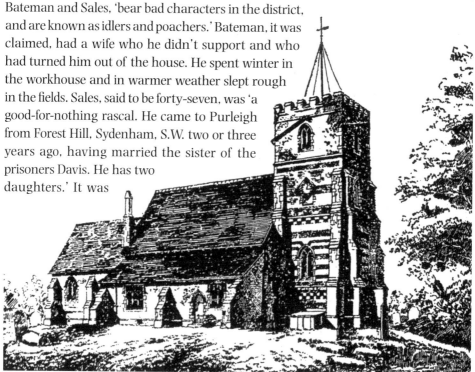

Purleigh Church, 1893.

also reported that Richard Davis had served nine months in prison for theft of turkeys.

On 24 April, at Maldon borough police court, the Davis brothers, Charles Sales, John Bateman and the Ramseys, all of whom had been held in Springfield Prison, were charged with the wilful murder of Sergeant Eves. Mr Seward Pearce of the solicitor's department conducted the prosecution. Elizabeth Eves was in court and before the justices had taken their seats she fainted and had to be revived with water. Mr J.W. Atkinson, appearing for Richard Davis, called attention to the *Essex County Chronicle* which had stated that the Davises had previous convictions, and challenged the whole police force of Essex to say that Richard was ever in a police court in his life. The chairman replied that the magistrates would not be influenced by what was in the newspapers. Elizabeth, dressed in deep mourning, gave evidence in a low voice, now and again bursting out into sobs. Sales, who was very vocal, declared loudly and often that he knew nothing about the murder.

Herbert Patten, who had found the body, told the court that he had seen Richard Davis on the Sunday at a quarter past four. Asked if he noticed anything unusual he said, 'I thought he looked bad – white.' He had also seen John talking to Sales. None of the witnesses, however, had seen Sales anywhere about the farm premises on Friday or Saturday.

John Moss, the bailiff, said that there was a little barley mixed in with the wheat stacked in the barn and the grain found in the Davises' house was similar. The production of the blood-smeared bludgeons caused a sensation in court, and Dr George Scott said the wounds might have been produced by them. Hair had been found clutched in the hands of the deceased, but it was impossible to indentify to whom it belonged. Scott had examined Ramsey in gaol and found some scratches on his back, but didn't think they could have been caused in a struggle. Ramsey had claimed that they were caused by part of an engine falling on him.

Edward Hunt Carter, surgeon at Chelmsford Prison, had examined the body and he believed that Eves had been attacked by at least two men. The prisoners were remanded for a week, and that afternoon the coroner's enquiry at the Moot Hall, Maldon, was also adjourned.

Meanwhile there was considerable concern over the fate of Eves' widow. The police authorities only had the power to grant her £15-a-year pension, so an additional levy was made on the members of the death fund and a further £21 was raised. An appeal was launched for more funds, and within three weeks almost £200 had poured in.

On Monday 1 May, the six prisoners were brought before the magistrates at the governor's office, Chelmsford Gaol. They listened to the evidence sullenly but said nothing. It transpired that none of the knives examined by the police could be shown to be the murder weapon. Labourers were still searching for it, but despite emptying ponds, and digging out the mud, nothing had been found.

Feelings were running high, and when the prisoners were taken from gaol to the Moot Hall for later hearings, large crowds assembled to see them. The *Essex Standard*

John Bateman.

reported that the crowds had been well behaved, but other newspapers suggested that there had been hostile demonstrations. On 8 May, at the resumed inquest, coroner John Harrison was obliged to dismiss a jury man who had tried to intimidate Thomas Choat.

At the magistrates' hearing on Monday 15 May there was drama in court when Bateman was discharged for lack of evidence and immediately entered the witness box. He said that when taken before the magistrates on 24 April, he had been waiting in a room adjoining the court and had had a conversation with Sales about what lawyer he might employ. According to Bateman, Sales had said, 'What is the use of me having a lawyer as I am a guilty man?' adding, 'What is the good of Richard Davis and John Davis having a lawyer? They are as guilty as I am.' Sales was incensed by this evidence and called out, 'It's shameful, shameful!'

Intimidation of the witness Choat and discovery of Sales hiding behind a hedge.

Dr Stevenson, the Home Office analyst, said that the blood with which the spade and sticks were smeared was mammalian. One stick had a human head hair on it. Hair found in Eves' left hand was from a beard coarser than his own, and the hair in the right hand was also from a beard. Judging from the appearance he doubted that the hair belonged to Richard Davis. All the prisoners were again remanded.

On 18 May, the final day of the inquest, the jury decided that while there was grave suspicion against the prisoners there was 'not enough to commit' and returned a verdict that Eves had been murdered 'by person or persons unknown.'

On 24 May at the Moot Hall, James Ramsey Jnr was discharged and the other four men were committed for trial at the Essex Assizes. On 18 July Mr R.J. Drake made an application before the Queen's Bench division to have the case removed to the Central Criminal Court, on the basis that it was impossible for the prisoners to receive a fair trial in Essex. He produced a copy of the *Essex County Chronicle* referring especially to page 6 of the issue of 21 April, in which there was an article headed 'Antecedents of the prisoners' which commented on their history and characters, and said that it was suspected that the men were involved in corn robberies. Three of the men, Sales, Ramsey and John Davis, had made an affidavit claiming that when being taken from Chelmsford Gaol to the magistrates' enquiry and coroner's inquisition crowds of people had assembled in the villages along the route 'who received them with hooting and hostile demonstration' such that it had become necessary to change the route of travel.

When the application was heard on 20 July, however, Mr Crump QC pointed out that the coroner's jury had not delivered a verdict against the prisoners, which showed that they could not have been influenced by the newspapers. Essex, he said, was a large county and precautions could be taken that no juryman would be drawn from the immediate neighbourhood.

Richard Davis denied that there had been any public hostility, and did not consent to the indictment being removed, but Mr Drake produced copies of the *Essex County Chronicle* and *Essex Weekly News*, both of which had referred to demonstrations against the prisoners.

Mr Justice Cave discharged the application. While deploring that any respectable newspaper should remark on the prisoners' antecedents, he noted that this had not influenced the coroner's jury. 'If that be so, much less will there be any prejudice when two months had elapsed.' He regretted that the prisoners' funds had been wasted in the application, as the money might have been better spent in preparing their defence.

The trial opened at Chelmsford Assizes on Wednesday 27 July before Mr Justice Mathew. On the second day, Mr Crump QC for the prosecution said that he did not think they ought to press the case further against Charles Sales. The judge agreed as there was no substantial evidence against Sales, and directed the jury to acquit him.

Medical evidence was given that wounds on the head of the deceased were caused by a sharp heavy weapon such as the spade belonging to the Davises. Just before the case for the prosecution was about to close, Mr Crump asked the judge to hear

James Ramsey Snr.

an application from him for the immediate adjournment of the trial until the evening, to allow time for the arrival of a new and important witness about whom he had only just heard and who it was believed could give vital evidence. The judge retired to his private room to hear the application, and on his return told the jury that the prisoners' counsel felt they could not strongly oppose the application and he had no doubt that in the interests of justice it was necessary to accede to the request and adjourn till 6 p.m. At 6 p.m. the judge again took his seat on the bench but Mr Crump said that the witness could not arrive in time and asked for an adjournment until the next day. This was granted.

The trial resumed on Saturday morning and the important witness appeared. She was Grace Davis, the thirteen-year-old niece of the Davis brothers, who had at the time of the murder lived with Richard Davis Snr his wife Elizabeth and Richard Jnr. Grace said that on 15 April she had gone to bed at half past 9 and her uncle Richard had also gone to bed. She had stayed in bed until 7 a.m. the next morning, and did not know if anyone had left the house during the night. When she got up her uncle Richard and grandfather were in the house. Asked what they were doing and what they said she replied that they were doing nothing and she could not hear them talking. Her uncle then went to put on his Sunday clothes and had breakfast at half past eight. Grace went to chapel, where she first heard about the murder. She returned and told her uncle, and they had all gone out together to see the place. She had seen her uncle John on the Sunday morning just before eight o clock and saw him again in the afternoon, when the police were at the house searching. Grace claimed that she did not hear anyone in her family talk about the terrible news. After the last magistrates' hearing she had been sent away to live with her mother in Middlesbrough. This closed the evidence.

The judge told the jury that it was 'clear beyond a doubt', that the men who had stolen the corn had murdered the sergeant. There had been a carefully planned robbery and the tally which was in the handwriting of Ramsey had been falsified. This stated that 14 quarters of corn had been threshed whereas two more had been threshed. He thought there was more evidence against the Davis brothers than Ramsey, and that '...as to the evidence of the little girl, they must consider whether she could have told more than she did.' The only thing of note was that, according to her statement, the brothers had said nothing about the case even after the murder had been discovered. The jury retired at half past three and returned at a quarter to five. They returned a verdict of guilty against the Davis brothers and found Ramsey not guilty. John said, 'I hope you will be merciful to me, my lord' and Richard said, 'I am innocent.' The judge passed sentence of death upon them both.

In August the brothers independently made confessions which agreed with each other. Richard Jnr told his father, who was visiting him in Chelmsford Gaol, that he and John had been involved in the theft of corn, and that his brother had knocked the sergeant down but that it was Ramsey who had cut the policeman's throat. John exonerated his brother from the murder. He said that Ramsey had committed the murder and he had assisted, but Richard, while helping to steal the grain, had not been present when Eves was killed. He had arrived on the scene afterwards and helped dispose of the body.

On 15 August, Richard Davis was reprieved and his sentence was reduced to life imprisonment. John, who was very penitent, was told of this and said, 'I am glad of it: it's the right thing.' He was executed at Chelmsford Gaol on the following day.

James Ramsey was re-arrested and charged with the theft of the grain. On 21 August he appeared before the Maldon bench and amongst the witnesses against him were Richard Davis, John's widow Selina, and bailiff John Moss. Ramsey was committed for trial at the next Essex Assizes. On the following day Ramsey, who was being held in Chelmsford Gaol, was considering his options and asked to see Mr Ward the chief warder, saying he wanted to make a statement as he had something on his mind. Ward cautioned the prisoner, who said, 'If I confess that I did the crime, I should confess what I never did. Richard Davis said that Eves died in a minute, but he and his brother were hacking at him for 15 minutes.' 'Then you were there steal-

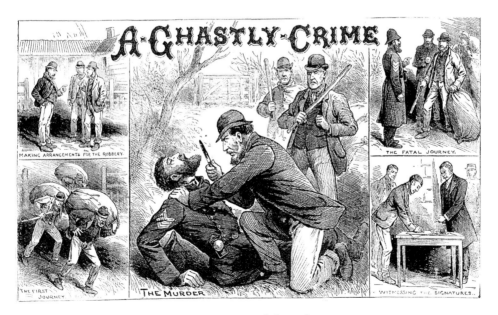

Scenes from the robbery and murder, and the signing of the confessions.

ing the corn,' said Ward. 'I am quite ready to take my punishment,' said Ramsey, adding after a moment's thought, 'Would a man be guilty if he was there with a horse and cart to carry away the corn and only looking on?'

James Ramsey was tried for the theft on 10 November 1893 before the Lord Chief Justice, Lord Coleridge.

With John Davis hanged and Richard in prison, witnesses were rather more forthcoming about the events of 15 April. Selina Davis said that she knew Ramsey and knew his voice well. On the night of the murder he had come to her house and fetched her husband away. She had gone to bed and later woke, hearing the voices of her husband and brother-in-law.

Selina was cross-examined by the prisoner, who was representing himself. Ramsey suggested that her husband had told her that he was at the barn (presumably at the time of the murder), but she denied it. He then suggested that she had heard her husband ask him to give evidence on his (John's) behalf if he was accused, whereupon he had asked John if he had anything to do with the murder, but she denied hearing any such conversation.

Richard Davis, brought from prison to give evidence, said that at 9.30 on 15 April he was at home and went to bed. Later, John came for him and he went to his brother's house, where he saw Ramsey. They took two sticks and six empty bags and went to the barn, which they found locked. They broke in, filled their sacks and carried them across the fields. He had gone first, followed by his brother, with Ramsey bringing up the rear. As he went he heard his brother call out twice and heard a scuffle. He went back and found his brother and Ramsey standing over the policeman, who was lying dead with his throat cut. 'You're a good sort of mate, Dick, aren't you?' said Ramsey, who seemed annoyed that Richard had not helped him. John admitted that he had held the policeman down while Ramsey cut his throat. 'Let's put him on the railway,' said Ramsey, but John said, 'No, let's put him in the ditch and go home.' They put the body in the ditch and went home, throwing part of the corn into a pond close by. On Monday his brother and Ramsey had both come to him and told him to keep his mouth shut, Ramsey promising that if he did so he would see that he had a lawyer.

Ramsey-cross examined in an effort to show that it was the Davis brothers who had committed the murder. He suggested that Richard had told him that the policeman had lain in agony for an hour and that

Mr Justice Coleridge.

they went home for a spade to bury him and found him still alive on their return. Richard denied this, saying the whole thing did not take more than a minute. 'I won't ask this man any more questions,' said Ramsey, angrily, 'He is a false man, and the country shall know it, even if I am put away innocent.'

Grace Davis now appeared and testified that on 15 April she had heard Ramsey call her uncle Richard to come out. She admitted that at the last assizes she had not spoken as she 'did not want to injure her uncles.' She now wished that she had spoken at the time, 'and then perhaps Ramsey would be in her Uncle John's shoes.'

With all the evidence in, Ramsey addressed the jury and said that he was innocent and all he knew of the matter was from the brothers Davis. The Lord Chief Justice summed up, pointing out that the pris-

Charles Sales.

oner was being tried solely on the charge of corn stealing. The law of England was that 'no man was to be twice vexed for the same cause' and as Ramsey had been acquitted of murder, no evidence that came to light afterwards could be used against him on that charge.

Ramsey was found guilty. Despite his words to the jury, Coleridge clearly intended that the murder of Eves should be a factor in Ramsey's punishment: '... while the law of England does not allow you to be again put on your trial for the horrible murder of which you were acquitted at the last assizes,' he said, 'there is nothing to prevent me from taking all the circumstances of the case into consideration when dealing with your crime. I should not be doing my duty if I shortened by one hour the punishment fixed by Act of Parliament for your crime.' Ramsey was sentenced to fourteen years in prison.

Despite his acquittal, Charles Sales felt obliged to leave Essex with his family. On 16 October 1893 he appeared before the Worship Street police court applying for assistance, saying he lived at Bow and he, his wife and two children were nearly starving and he could not get work. He was a watch and clock jobber and repairer but had also done labouring and farm work. His home had been sold to pay for his defence and he had been living on help from relatives. For the last week he had subsisted on nothing but bread. He was given temporary assistance, and it was later reported that a gentlemen had found a paid situation for him.

In 1901 Richard Davis was in Parkhurst Gaol, and James Ramsey in Portland convict prison, Dorset. Both were eventually freed. Ramsey died in 1940, aged eighty-seven.

5

'WHERE IS FLORRIE?'

Prittlewell, 1894

James Canham Read was a liar, adulterer, thief and ultimately a murderer who brought disgrace and tragedy to the lives he touched.

Born in 1857, the son of an upholsterer, Read aspired to white-collar employment and cultivated a gentlemanly appearance. Initially a pupil teacher he rejected this profession as too lowly paid, and in November 1874 he became a shipping clerk. On 1 July 1877 he married eighteen-year-old Emma Sarah Payne; their first child was already on the way and a daughter was born on 20 October.

Read was a competent and reliable employee who rose to become paymaster at the Royal Albert Docks, a position of trust in which he had charge of the keys of three safes. In 1891 his annual salary was £140, and additional work as an insurance agent brought his total income to £200. By then he was the father of seven children and although to all outward appearances he was a good husband and parent, Read did not let his substantial domestic responsibilities get in the way of the obsession which was to be his downfall – the pursuit and seduction of young women. His double life required unflagging energy, not a little expenditure and considerable guile if he was to remain undiscovered, but his greatest talent was to be plausible. The principal clerk at the Docks later described him as 'a quiet, peaceable and respectable man' who was well liked by his fellow clerks. 'Read,' said the *Essex County Standard,* 'is a sober, educated and intelligent man, and was believed to be of exemplary character.'

In August 1889 Read met twenty-four-year-old dairyman's wife Louise Ayriss (*née* Dennis) on Southend Pier. There was an immediate mutual attraction and for Louise perhaps the thrill of an illicit adventure. Read lost no time in making an assignation and together they went on a trip to Rayleigh the very next day. They continued to meet about twice a month and Read wrote to Louise, addressing the letters to 'Mrs Neville.' Louise had four younger sisters: Emma, who married Alfred Dee in 1891,

Florence, born in 1871, who was single, and the youngest Evelina and Lily, still at school. Florence led a humdrum existence in which she appeared to have no occupation either for hands or mind, and spent some of her time living with her parents and some with her married sisters.

Louise and her husband John lived in Wandsworth, and it was there in the autumn of 1890 that Florence was out walking with Emma when they encountered Louise in the company of James Canham Read. An introduction took place and the opportunistic Read walked on with Florence for a while. The correspondence between Read and Louise Ayriss continued until March 1892, when it ceased, under circumstances which were later to be hotly disputed.

The Ayriss family moved to Kingston-upon-Thames and in May 1892 Louise gave birth to her second son. Florence was helping look after Louise and the new baby, and asked the nurse in attendance to post letters for her, making her promise not to tell her sister about them. They were addressed to 'Mr Read, Albert Docks'.

In August 1892 Florence was absent from her sister's home for one night, something which was never explained. In the following month Louise found a letter in Florence's skirt addressed to a 'Miss Latimer' at the Ayriss's old Wandsworth address, St John Hill. 'My dear girl,' it read, 'I regret very deeply that I cannot keep my appointment. I quite expected that I should have the leisure of seeing you.' Louise recognised Read's handwriting and tackled Florence about it, but Florence laughed it off and told Louise she had picked up the letter and it wasn't for her.

In May 1893 Louise and her family moved to Hanwell and Florence went with them. The correspondence with Read continued. On 1 June Florence went to Sheerness, where she stayed with her parents at 44 Marine Parade. Not daring to have Read write to her there, she persuaded Emma, who also lived in Sheerness, to receive letters for her. Letters arrived for Florence in the name of 'Talbott' but when Emma's husband saw them and discovered what they were he refused to accept any more such letters at the house. Read then wrote to 'Miss Talbott' via a stationer's called Rigg's in Sheerness High Street. Mrs Rigg must have become suspicious, for she later refused to allow her house to be used for this purpose and a new address had to be found. The 'Miss Talbott' letters were then addressed care of Sheerness post office and Florence sent fourteen-year-old Evelina to collect them for her.

It was a busy time for Read. On 13 June his wife gave birth to their eighth child. Florence remained in Sheerness until 20 September 1893, when she went to stay with Louise in Hanwell. In October Louise visited her mother, leaving Florence to look after the house. If the affair between Florence and Read had not begun before it certainly began then, for in that month she became pregnant. In November, Florence was back at Sheerness, returning to Hanwell on 1 December, where she stayed until Christmas. She returned to Sheerness after Christmas and Read sent her telegrams arranging meetings. When Florence told Read that she was pregnant, she found to her distress that he was not in a position to marry her. Read promised to help her on condition that she did not name him as the father, threatening that if she did so he would deny responsibility. He instructed that if her parents found out about her condition she was to tell them that she had been waylaid by strangers.

On 19 June 1894, Florence finally confessed to her mother that she was pregnant and also revealed who the father was. The Dennis family were said to be 'of enthusiastically religious tendencies' and Mrs Dennis, not wanting Florence to give birth in a house where there were impressionable younger siblings, decided that it would be best to send her away. Mrs Dennis took Florence to live with Louise, who had recently moved house again, to Wesley Road, Southend. She had a cool reception, especially from John Ayriss, who was not happy about Florence giving birth in his house. Louise told her mother about the correspondence between Florence and Read and it was agreed that Read should be made to meet his obligations. Mrs Dennis went to the Sheerness telegraph office and collected Read's most recent telegram which she sent to Florence, who received it on 21 June. No doubt under the advice of her sister and mother, Florence wrote a letter to Read which read, 'Dear Sir, I have left Sheerness and am staying at Southend. Please write what arrangements you have made. Address Miss Dennis, at the Post-office, Southend.'

On 23 June Louise collected a telegram from Read to Florence, making an appointment to see him at 9 p.m. at the railway station that night. Florence returned from the meeting in a more cheerful mood, it having been agreed that they would meet again on Sunday, when he would tell her what arrangements would be made for her and the child.

What Florence and her family did not know was that Read had another mistress. On 16 October 1892 he had met twenty-six-year-old confectioner's assistant Miss Beatrice Diver Kempton at Gloucester Road railway station; no doubt his good manners enabled him to strike up a conversation without arousing suspicion. Read wasted no time in making an appointment to see her again. He told Beatrice that his name was Edgar Benson, that he was a single man, and a commercial traveller for Peek brothers, a firm of tea merchants. He gave his address as 16 North Street, Poplar.

A regular correspondence, a promise of marriage and a seduction followed. Read visited Beatrice at her home, and many meetings took place at railway stations. Beatrice was not invited to visit the Poplar address, which was the workplace of Read's younger brother Harry. Harry Victor Read, born in 1863, was a ne'er do well who preferred idling away his time with drinking and smoking to working for a living. He was very attached to his elder brother and was happy to be an accessory to his infidelities. In December Harry was dismissed from his job in Poplar for misconduct. Drinking hard, and in low spirits, he bought a revolver which used a type of cartridge known as a 7-Eley pinfire. It was obvious to his family that it was unsafe for Harry to own the revolver and Read took it away from him.

Read gave Beatrice a new correspondence address, 324 Mile End Road, which he said was the address of 'Harry Edwards' and his sister Flo'. It was actually a stationer's shop, whose owner had agreed to receive letters. Read used to call in twice a week to collect letters and sometimes Harry went instead.

Early in 1893, Beatrice took Read to meet her parents, who lived in Cambridge, and told them that they were engaged. In April, Read introduced Beatrice to his brother, saying that this was his friend 'Harry Edwards'. That summer, Read went to even greater lengths to cover his tracks, getting Beatrice to write to her parents using the High Street, Sheerness address and also a Clapham address, when they were actually staying at Hallingbury near Bishops Stortford as husband and wife. He asked Beatrice to tell her parents the next time she saw them that she had been staying with Harry and Flo Edwards in Sheerness and at a Mr Johnson's in Clapham, and she complied.

In August Miss Kempton realised that she was pregnant and asked Read if he would marry her. He said he couldn't just then as he did not want her condition to be known, but promised he would marry her after the child was born.

Meanwhile Beatrice's father, a retired printer aged eighty-one, who had distrusted Read at their first meeting, had decided to check up on 'Mr Edgar Benson' at Peek Brothers and was told that they had never heard of him. When Read was confronted with this, he said that Mr Kempton must have gone to the wrong place, and in any case he had just left. Beatrice returned to Hallingbury for her confinement, and at Read's suggestion told her parents that she had gone to be a lady's companion. While there, Read showed Beatrice the revolver; perhaps it was to impress her, or maybe it was a subtle threat; saying that he had to carry it while on the lonely road from Hallingbury to the railway station. Their son 'Bertie' was born in January 1894. Read did not marry Beatrice, but in order to satisfy her parents he gave her a forged marriage certificate, which purported to show that they had married on 19 March 1893.

In February Read rented Rose Cottage, Fair Green, Mitcham under the name of Benson and he, Miss Kempton and their child lived there. He used to stay with them from Saturday to Monday morning most weeks.

On the occasions when he was unable to be there he told her he was visiting a sister at Canterbury. On weekdays, when Miss Kempton thought he was working as a commercial traveller, Read was working at the Royal Albert Docks, and living with his wife and children at 57 Jamaica Street, Mile End. He explained his weekend absences by telling his wife he had a heart condition which he was afraid would kill him, and needed to spend weekends away to recuperate so he could do his week's work. At the same time, he was maintaining a correspondence with the pregnant Florence.

Read was making plans, although not the ones Florence and her family were anticipating. He wrote to Beatrice on Friday 22 June to say he could not see her on Saturday as usual as he had to go to Canterbury that weekend to deal with some critical financial matters. That Saturday he was at home with his wife and children, but sent a telegram to Florence, left, and did not return. The revolver which had been kept under a couch was later found to be missing.

Read may well have met with Florence on the afternoon of Sunday 24 June, for at three o'clock a Mrs Rebecca Kirby of Prittlewell, a village just to the north of Southend, was walking along a footpath that skirted a wheat field when a man and woman walking together overtook her. She was returning at half past four and saw the man alone.

Read engaging apartments and a sketch of Rose Cottage

He stopped her and asked the way to Leigh, which lay west of Prittlewell. She was unable to tell him and he said, 'I may as well go back to Rayleigh again then', turned around and walked quickly away. He had a quick active walk, and when he spoke to her he stood very close and she noticed his intense piercing eyes.

On the night of Sunday 24 June Louise had lodgers staying, and arranged that Florence would sleep at nearby 37 Stanley Road, a lodging house run by a Mrs Susannah Eggers. Florence went out shortly before 9 p.m., but although she called at Mrs Eggers' house she only stayed there a quarter of an hour and went away. At a quarter past eleven Mrs Eggers sent her servant, Fanny Philpott, to Louise's house to ask after Florence and found that she was not there. Mrs Eggers waited up for Florence until a quarter past two, but she did not appear.

There was one possible sighting of Florence that night. A little after 10 p.m., umbrella maker Robert Douthwaite was walking from Prittlewell towards Gainsborough Avenue when he saw a man and a woman walking together arm-in-arm, on the road near the vicarage, engaged in animated conversation. When near the entrance to the fields leading to the vicarage they turned abruptly. The man seemed to wheel the woman around to go across the field, an action which took her by surprise as she had wanted to continue down the road.

Richard Golding was a gas worker of Southend. That Sunday just after half past 10, he, his wife and daughter were walking along the Leigh road and when near Gainsborough Avenue he saw a man abruptly emerge from the Prittlewell side of the road and walk off in the direction of Leigh at a rapid pace.

At 1 a.m. the next morning, Police Constable Daniels, stationed at Southend, was standing at the corner of a street at Benfleet, which is just beyond Leigh, when he saw a man coming from the direction of Southend. 'You are up and dressed early this morning,' he said. The man asked the policeman the way to Benfleet, saying he wanted the road to London. Daniels gave the man directions and he walked briskly away, but in the few minutes they talked the constable was able to observe the man's face.

That morning, at about 9.20 a.m., Read called briefly at the Leytonstone home of a fellow clerk called Scannell, who was ill. The normally smart and fresh looking Read was uncharacteristically unshaven, worn and dishevelled. He did not arrive at his work until 10 a.m., but since he had previously been asked to visit Scannell to check when he might be fit to return to his duties, his explanation for lateness was accepted.

Early that same morning Louse Ayriss had gone to Mrs Eggars' to check on Florence and was told that her sister had not returned to stay the night. When John Ayriss returned from the dairy at 8.30 a.m., Florence was still not home. Louise went to the police station to report her sister as missing, and gave a description of both Florence and Read. John Ayriss then wrote a telegram to Read at his work address and took it the post office. The message read 'Where is Florrie?' and was delivered at about 3 p.m. Read's reply showed that he was unaware that Florence had confided in her family. 'What is the meaning of your extraordinary wire? Please write fully. I have not seen this young person for quite 18 months when you were at St John's Hill.'

Despite the assured tone of his reply, Read was rattled. He realised that the search was on for Florrie and it was only a matter of time before she was found. There was just one place to which he could go, the one address not known to Mrs Ayriss; Rose Cottage, Mitcham. He wrote to his brother, 'My dear Harry, Secure my desk and contents and report everything to me at M – in strict secrecy. Will explain all when I see you and allay all fears.'

Hastily, he started burning any incriminating papers, most probably the many letters and telegrams he had received from Florence. Mr Edwin Burgess an employee at the Royal Albert Docks, was passing Read's office and saw a large fire in the grate. It was a hot summer's day so he asked Read what he was doing. Read hesitated and suggested there was a bad smell and he was 'trying to burn the air out.' Read left the office about five minutes before his normal time of 4 p.m., without signing out as he usually did.

He arrived at Mitcham looking fatigued and told Miss Kempton that he had been to his sister in Canterbury. He said that the accounts at his office had been found to be wrong and he was not going back. Beatrice must have been appalled and anxious, but had no choice but to support him.

At half past five that evening Frederick Rush of 17 Royal Terrace Southend was walking along a footpath through a wheatfield a few hundred yards from Prittlewell. A hedge ran along the side of the path and on the other side of the hedge was a deep ditch, some 7ft wide, and another field of wheat. Rush saw a gap in the hedge as if something had been pushed through it. There was a pool of blood on the ground and a trail across the grass leading to the ditch on the edge of which lay a woman's glove. Peering into the ditch Rush saw the body of a young woman lying doubled up.

Rush went at once to Southend police station and Sergeant Marden hurried to the spot, closely followed by Superintendent Hawtree and Inspector Chase. It appeared that the victim had been murdered in the middle of a neighbouring field near to the vicarage, and dragged to the brook. The body was taken to a shed at the back of the nearby Spread Eagle Inn.

At 6.30 p.m. that evening, Louise Ayriss was informed that a body had been found, and was taken to the Spread Eagle, where she identified her sister. The body was later seen by Mr Douthwaite, who was sure it was that of the young woman he had seen walking with a man on Sunday night.

Dr Avery Clough Waters, a general practitioner of Southend, was called to examine the body. He arrived at about 8 p.m. and estimated that Florence had been dead some 15 to 20 hours. On the left side of the head, just in front of the ear, there was a large circular gunshot wound. The edges of the wound were blackened, showing that the gun had been held close to her head. At the post-mortem held the following morning a bullet was found in the brain. The weapon was not found but was thought to be a 7-Eley firing a pin cartridge. Death would have been instantaneous.

James Canham Read was the only suspect in the murder, and his description was circulated: about 5ft 4in tall, and of a gentlemanly appearance, with a fresh complexion, light brown moustache, and 'fine, full eyes.' He was dressed in a black coat and waistcoat with light grey trousers and a brown hard felt hat. When Read didn't turn up to work on the Tuesday morning, duplicate keys were obtained for the three safes he usually had under his control and when they were opened it was discovered that there was a deficiency of almost £160.

The inquest on Florence opened at the Spread Eagle on 27 June, where Louise Ayriss told the court that she had seen Read in Southend waiting outside the railway station at 9 p.m. on Sunday 24 June. She had gone home and told Florence, who went out to meet him at 9.15. p.m.

On 28 June the police went to 57 Jamaica Street. Mrs Read was not initially told of the seriousness of the charge. She said she had not seen her husband since Saturday morning and the revolver which she had seen in a drawer three weeks ago was missing. The house was kept under observation and the police saw Harry Read visit,

Superintendent Hawtree.

66

THE SOUTHEND MYSTERY.

The discovery of the body of Florence Dennis.

and noticed that after he left the distraught wife was more cheerful. Harry obviously knew something and the police obtained permission to intercept any mail delivered to him.

That morning, Read was trying to change his appearance. He went to Croydon with Miss Kempton and bought a light-coloured suit and a straw hat. Thereafter he did not wear the old suit and hat again. Normally clean-shaven, he allowed his beard to grow. Beatrice, who must have assumed that any change in his habits and demeanour was were due to financial worries, asked him several times why he did not shave and he said that he was tired. Anxious that the police were on his trail, Read went away and was absent for two nights. On 29 June Beatrice received a telegram. 'Mrs Benson. Wire immediately if all serene; preserve letters unopened.' A telegram was sent in reply that all was well and he returned.

On 30 June the funeral of Florence Dennis took place at St John's Church Southend. On 7 July the police learned that Harry Read had written a letter to a Mr Benson of Rose Cottage, Mitcham. Detective Inspector Charles Frederick Baker of the CID, Scotland Yard, and Sergeant Marden of the Essex County Constabulary went to Rose Cottage. 'Benson' came to the door and denied that he was James Canham Read, but undeterred, Baker said that he was under arrest for the murder of Florence Dennis. 'You are on the wrong scent,' said Read. He tried to get something from his pocket, but was promptly searched and Baker found a razor on him and removed it. He was also carrying £50 and a newspaper report of the murder and inquest. Miss Kempton told Inspector Baker that the man in custody was her husband, Edgar Benson, and showed him the forged marriage certificate. Shortly afterwards Harry Read arrived at the house and was questioned. It was only then that Miss Kempton discovered that 'Harry Edwards' was Read's brother.

On his way to the railway station Read, who had dropped all pretence of being Benson, told his escort, 'Mrs Ayriss knows more about it than I, she can tell you where the revolver is. This about Southend is all rot. I was considering whether I should attend the inquest and offer to give evidence.' He was taken by train from Mitcham to Victoria and thence to Fenchurch Street Station for a train to Southend. The news of the arrest had preceded them for at Southend a large crowd had assembled at the station, which was guarded by police. Read was taken to the police station in a cab, which was followed by a crowd, hissing, hooting and yelling 'Lynch him!' At the station, Superintendent Hawtree read over a warrant to the prisoner. Read made no reply.

When the police searched Rose Cottage they found some letters in a box which bore dates between November 1892 and June 1894. Some were from 324 Mile End Road and some from 16 North Road, Poplar.

The police informed Emma Read of her husband's arrest and she came to see him on the Sunday. She was reported to be 'indignant' with her husband for his infidelities, although she believed he was innocent of murder. The newspapers reported that there were two other women with whom Read had been intimate and who had thought he was single.

Miss Kempton was prostrate with grief, and it was some days before she recovered enough to leave the cottage. Fortunately, her parents said they they would be willing to take her back to live with them and look after both her and the child.

On 9 July, PC Daniels identified Read as the man to whom he had given directions. Richard Golding was brought to the police station and identified Read as the man he

Read and 'Mrs Benson'.

ARREST OF READ

The arrest of James Canham Read.

Superintendent Hawtree. (Courtesy of the Essex Police Museum)

had seen on the night of the murder. Douthwaite had not seen the face of the man walking with Florence, but on 12 July he selected Read from a line-up because of his walk and bearing. Mrs Kirby was able to identify Read as the man she had spoken to on Sunday afternoon. She said she had remembered him well because he came up to her 'in a peculiar manner', coming very close as he faced her.

On 16 July, Read, described in the newspapers as 'a handsome and stylish man, of smart address and bearing', made his first appearance at Southend police court. On 22 July the police went to Read's home in Stepney where they broke open a desk and found a dozen blank forms purporting to be marriage certificates.

When Miss Kempton was called to give evidence at the next hearing on 30 July, she was in such a state of distress that she was unable to answer the questions put to her and had to be removed from the court in the company of a female attendant. After an absence of three quarters of an hour she returned, whereupon Read gazed at her so intently that she again burst into tears, but eventually recovered enough to tell her story.

On 13 August Mrs Ayriss was cross-examined at some length by Mr Warburton, the barrister acting for Read's defence, about the nature of her correspondence with Read. There was a sensation in court when she admitted that she had been to the Lyric Theatre with him. She freely stated that she had received telegrams from him and had corresponded with him over a period of four years, but that this was on both business and personal matters. She had taken the financial advice of a stranger in preference to that of her husband because 'he did not look after the business as he ought to have done.' She said she had met Read on a number of occasions as she was going to take another house and she thought he could recommend his friends to lodge there. She also claimed that it was she and not he who had broken off the correspondence. It might not have been apparent at that time, but it later became clear that Warburton was hoping to introduce some doubt into the jury's mind by suggesting that Louise had motive to tell lies about Read.

John Ayriss had entered the court that day with no idea that his wife had had any communication with Read, and the revelations must have come as a shock. A few days later it was reported that he had sent his children away from Southend and had given instructions that the Wesley Road property should be sold up.

At the resumed hearing on 18 August, both Louise and her husband were present but sat apart and did not appear to recognise each other. Louise was cross- examined by Warburton at some length and admitted that she had had a great many letters and telegrams from Read, which were 'both of a friendly and business character.' Warburton asked if she had been to Buckingham and stayed at a house there with Read as husband and wife. Faced with that information, Louise admitted that she had. He asked whether she had passed as Read's wife at a house in Leigh and she admitted that too. From the body of the court, her husband hissed loudly. She was adamant that it was she who had broken off the relationship and not Read, telling him that she was not going to see him or write to him any more. Despite this she had later gone to his home in Stepney in the company of her mother, taking her child with her. Asked the reason for the visit, she told the court she had gone to consult

*Mrs Ayriss in court and the sale of
the home of the Ayriss family.*

with him about a lease on a house, as he had been advising her on legal and business matters. Warburton suggested that she had gone there to make a scene because Read had refused to see her. She denied this most emphatically.

One thing was very clear to the court – Louise had been the only person in a position to warn Florence about Read, yet she had failed to protect her sister. Louise claimed that Florence had been under the impression that Read was divorced, but when challenged was unable to say on what grounds she might have thought this. Finally she admitted that she had never told Florence that Read was a married man. The best explanation she could offer was 'because I thought I would keep a sharp lookout as to what they were doing.' Louise's motives are unclear but she may still have had an interest in Read and wanted to keep an eye on him. Worse was to follow.

Louise Ayriss was again brought before the court and made a damaging admission. She had earlier made a deposition to the effect that she had seen Read in Southend on Sunday 24 June, the night of the murder. She now confessed to the court that she had lied. She had not been out that night at all. She said she had invented the story because she was sure that Read had been in Southend that night. No other part of her evidence was untrue, she added.

Harry Read was called to the witness stand, but failed to appear and a warrant was issued for his arrest. Read was taken to Chelmsford Gaol to await the adjourned hearing. To avoid a repetition of the disturbances at Southend station, he was driven from the court to Rochford two stations further up the line.

On 31 August thirty-one-year-old Harry Victor Read appeared in court. He described himself as an insurance agent and was staying with a friend in Whitechapel. He knew about his brother's philandering and had heard him refer to Mrs Ayriss as 'the little dairymaid'. Harry had played an active role in the deceptions, collecting correspondence, passing on letters and addressing envelopes. He described his being introduced to Miss Kempton as Harry Edwards as 'a joke.' He confirmed that there was no sister living in Canterbury. He had last seen James on the Friday before the murder and had no idea as to where his brother was on the Saturday and Sunday nights. The note from James dated 25 June was read out in court and Harry admitted that after receiving it, he had gone to his brother's house, broken open his desk and secured the contents. He claimed he did not know what 'M' stood for.

The forged certificate of marriage between Miss Kempton and Read was produced in court and Harry said he knew nothing about it. Read was committed for trial and assured the court of his 'perfect innocence', claiming that last June he had not seen Florence for eighteen months. The trial of James Canham Read opened at the Chelmsford Assizes on 12 November before Baron Pollock. The voluminous amount of evidence in the case meant that each of the briefs was estimated by observers as a cubic foot of paper. Much of the trial was taken up with examination of handwriting on the many letters and telegrams sent by Read, but the defence, seizing upon Louise Ayriss's lies, was eager to insinuate that the correspondence sent to Florence had actually been meant for Louise, and tried to get her to admit that Florence had 'got into trouble with a soldier', which Louise denied.

The defence counsel, Mr Cock QC, brought no witnesses, relying on his summing up of the case. He suggested that Louise had lied throughout and that her relationship with Read had continued after March 1892, even stating as a fact (for which there was no proof) that both Louise's sons were Read's children. He thought that the handwriting evidence was 'not worth discussing' and cast doubts on the accuracy of the identification of the eyewitnesses who had seen Read on the road. He maintained that there was no evidence that Florence had been seduced by Read and suggested that Florence had got into the family way by a soldier at Hanwell. The only explanation the defence could offer as to Read's whereabouts on the fatal night cannot have endeared Read to the jury. Mr Cock suggested that Read was with a woman, and was planning to abandon Miss Kempton for another mistress.

The jurymen must have formed a very firm opinion of the character of James Canham Read, although the judge in his summing up urged them to dismiss from their minds the 'immoral and licentious conduct' of the accused. Since there was no witness to the murder, it was, he said, for the jury to make up their minds if the accumulated evidence 'pointed irresistibly to a conclusion of guilt.' It took the jury just half an hour to return a verdict of guilty. Asked if he had anything to say,

James Canham Read in prison.

Read told the court that he was perfectly innocent, had not seen Florence in two years and had never written to her. He claimed that Louise had written telling him that Florence 'had got into trouble with a soldier at Hanwell.' Adding that on the fatal night he had been 50 miles away from the spot where the murder was committed, he folded his arms and sat down. The judge put on the black cap and said that the evidence could 'leave no doubt in the mind of any person present in court who heard it', and passed sentence of death.

Emma Read forgave her husband his infidelities and visited him in prison as often as she could, continuing to hope that new evidence would be discovered to save him. With no financial support she faced the prospect of her children being taken from her, and had been working in a laundry from five or six in the morning to between midnight and one o'clock the next morning in order to feed her family. By the end of the trial the anxiety and exhaustion had left her a crushed woman. A public subscription was opened for her.

John Ayriss wrote an extraordinary letter to Read, informing him that Miss Kempton's father had recently passed away. While believing that Read deserved to be hanged, he had his own ideas of a suitable punishment. 'I would lock you up in a dark Dungen as long as you lived and fetch you out once a month and give you the *Cat* of about 30 strokes and I would like to be the one who would give it to you.'

Harry visited his brother in prison and found him confident of a reprieve. Read assured Harry that he was innocent. He had petitioned the Home Office, stating that there were witnesses who could say that he was in bed at a lodging house, 1 Gresham Villas, Southend from 11 p.m. on the night of Sunday 24 June to

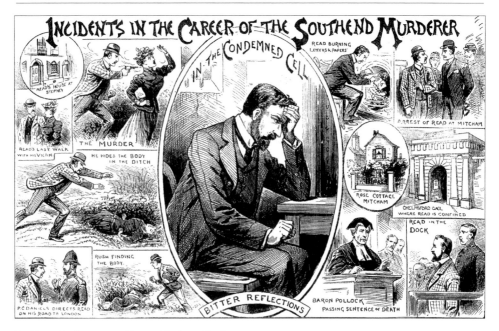

Incidents in the career of James Canham Read.

7 a.m. the next morning, while the medical evidence showed that Florence had died between 12 a.m. and 5 a.m. He was unaware that the police had interviewed the lodging house keeper, who recognised Read from a portrait, but as someone who had breakfasted there on the Sunday, the morning before the murder and not the morning after. The Home Secretary did not grant the petition.

Read never confessed to his crime. He was a master deceiver and managed to deceive himself to the end. On Sunday 2 December he wrote to his brother stating 'in spite of the truth and in defiance of the evidence presented to him proving my innocence, the Home Secretary has endorsed the murderous conspiracy of his professional brethren.' He claimed that there were further proofs of his innocence 'which the neglect of my legal representatives kept from Judge and jury.'

A haggard-looking Read was led to the scaffold on the morning of Tuesday 4 December. The only comment he made in his final moments was to ask the executioner to button his coat.

Harry took his brother's death badly. Since the execution he had little employment and spent his days mainly in smoking and drinking. On Thursday, 7 May 1896, his body was found in the Regent's Canal. He was thirty-two.

John and Louise Ayriss were eventually reconciled and opened a new dairy. Beatrice changed her surname to Kaye and she and her son lived with her widowed mother. In 1903 she married fifty-year-old widower Frederic Powis, who died in the following year. In 1899 Emma Read married Herbert Strickland, who was seven years her junior and by whom she already had a two-year-old daughter.

6

MURDER IN HONEYPOT LANE

Basildon, 1906

In 1906, Basildon, Billericay, Pitsea, Woodham Ferrers and Fambridge were known as the 'bungalow districts' of South Essex. Some bungalow dwellers worked in the city but liked a rural retreat for the weekend, some were permanent residents; market gardeners or labourers employed locally; while others tilled a smallholding raising crops and livestock, aiming as far as possible at self-sufficiency.

Honeypot Lane was a 2-mile-long grassy cart track about 5 miles from Billericay and 3 or 4 from Pitsea, linking the Billericay and Southend road to the east and the Stanford and Vange road to the west. The nearest houses were about a quarter of a mile away. There was no water supply to the bungalows in the lane, and residents had to collect rainwater in butts and tubs for drinking, and water their livestock from ponds.

Early in 1906, forty-seven year old Albert Watson and his fifty-year-old wife Emma, came to occupy a bungalow in this remote spot where they ran a poultry farm. Watson had been a carpenter in Kilburn, and having saved a little money, decided to retire to the peace of the countryside. Their home was a two-room dwelling with a shed at the back. The Watsons were a sober and respectable couple, regular attendees of the Basildon Mission Chapel. They worked hard and kept their modest home neat and clean, intending in time to replace the bungalow with a house. The couple had two sons; twenty-year-old Albert lived in Canada and Samuel Archibald, almost nineteen, was in the Royal Navy, stationed at Plymouth. The Watsons soon integrated into the social life of the area. Mr Watson preached at the Mission Chapel and the couple invited friends to their home for tea.

Their nearest neighbours were the Buckham family who lived at Sawyers Farm, and owned seven of its 26 acres. Richard and Margaret Buckham had previously lived in Bromley-by-Bow. They acquired the land in 1903, and spent weekends there, only coming to live on the property in March 1905. They occupied a brick-built bungalow on Honeypot Lane together with their sons. twenty-year-old Robert and Richard, seventeen, and four daughters. Buckham continued to work as an engineer, leaving home at 6 a.m. every weekday, travelling to Old Ford, London by the early train from Laindon station about 3.5 miles away, and returning at about 7.20 p.m. His sons cultivated the land, and looked after the livestock; a horse, four heifers, sheep, pigs and poultry. In 1904 Mr Buckham, Richard and a friend had dug a pond, which the family used to water the cattle. It measured 6 by 10ft and was surrounded by bushes and shaded by the overhanging branches of trees. In August 1906, however, due to a spell of dry weather there was only about twelve inches of water in one corner of the pond.

The Watsons had been getting water for their poultry from a pond belonging to farmer and dairyman Thomas Frederick Stevens. Stevens had come from West Ham to set up his business in Basildon some eight years previously. He was a busy, energetic man and he and his family, who occupied Lavender Cottage, were said to 'rejoice in their work and in the pure air of the countryside.' In mid August Mr Stevens' pond dried up. The Watsons asked Richard Buckham Snr if they could get water from his pond and he gave them permission. Robert Buckham noticed the Watsons taking water from their pond and mentioned it to his father who replied 'Let them take it.'

At about 6.05 a.m. on Thursday 23 August, Richard Buckham Snr started out for work, walking up the lane to the station. On the way he met gardener Edward Clayton and asked him the right time. Clayton replied that it was a quarter past six and Buckham walked on. About three minutes later Clayton heard two shots in rapid succession and then a cry of 'Oh! Oh! Oh!' Shortly afterwards he heard a third shot and another cry, and then all was silent. He assumed it was someone shooting rabbits.

A Mr Hughes and a horseman called Smith also heard the shots and cries. Neither of them attached any importance to them. At 6.30 Mr Stevens, whose land adjoined that of the Buckhams, passed by the Watsons' bungalow and noticed that the front door was open. He continued on to his home. At 7.57 the postman, Percy Ockenden, tried to deliver a package to the Watsons' bungalow, but was surprised to find the door shut and the blinds down. He was used to seeing the Watsons in the house or garden at that time in the morning but no-one was about.

At half past 10, Richard Buckham Jnr arrived at Lavender Cottage and told Mrs Stevens that he had found the Watsons lying dead in his pond and there was blood on Mr Watson's shirt. Mrs Stevens sent for her husband and told her son to go to Billericay for the police and a doctor, while Richard hurried off towards the top of Honeypot Lane to find Mr Stevens. He soon encountered the dairyman and told him of the discovery.

Richard said he had been taking his cattle to get water from the pond on his father's land and had found the Watsons dead. Stevens also sent someone for help and hurried to the spot with his neighbour. On the way they met Robert Buckham, who looked very agitated and seemed to have been crying. 'Have they moved?' asked Stevens. 'I think Mrs Watson has turned,' said Robert. At the pond Stevens saw Mr Watson lying with his body partly submerged in the water. He immediately jumped down and pulled him out. Watson was dead, his body already beginning to stiffen. Mrs Watson was lying face downwards on the dry part of the pond. There was blood on the clay near where the dead woman lay and blood on her face and hands. The dress at the nape of her neck was torn as if she had been pulled along by it. Beneath her was a pail, and nearby there was another pail and a bath in which the water was presumably to have been carried home. Both bodies were fully clothed and there was no sign of a struggle. Mrs Watson's hat, which was dry and clean, lay nearby. Stevens quickly satisfied himself that Mrs Watson was dead and left the bodies where they were and waited for help to arrive. He also noticed fresh blood marks in the adjoining field.

Revd H Carpenter, described by the *Essex Herald* as 'the energetic Rector of Laindon-cum-Basildon always ready to lend a helping hand in any emergency', who lived only half a mile from the Watsons' bungalow, was sent for. By the time he arrived there were already about a dozen people at the scene. He and Stevens went to the Watsons' home, finding the front door open and the key in the lock. They looked in and saw that the interior was in disorder. Carpenter locked the door and handed the key to Stevens.

The first policeman to arrive was constable Layzell of Billericay, who sent for local physician Dr Cresswell. Stevens showed him the blood marks in the field, told him the exact position of the bodies when he found them, and handed over the key

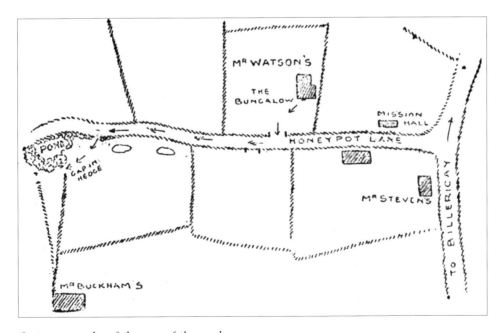

Contemporary plan of the scene of the murder.

The discovery of the bodies of Mr and Mrs Watson.

The Watsons' house.

Mrs Emma Watson.

to the bungalow. Layzell questioned the Buckham brothers, who said that they had found the bodies shortly after 10 a.m., then decided to move the bodies to the bungalow, and did so with the help of Mr Hughes, Stevens and Richard Jnr.

Stevens' first thought on finding the bodies was that there had been a murder followed by suicide, but when he saw a gaping wound on Albert Watson's back, he realised that it could not have been self-inflicted. Richard Buckham Jnr said little, but agreed with Stevens that the couple must both have been murdered and suggested the name of a man who 'might have done it.'

Superintendent Alfred Marden, who was in charge of the Brentwood police station, dispatched Sergeant Giggins and other constables to Honeypot Lane. The police dragged the pond but were unable to find a weapon, and spent a great deal of time raking through hedges and searching the surrounding fields.

Giggins asked to see the Buckhams' gun and Richard Jnr brought it out to him. It was a double-barrelled breech loading shotgun. The sergeant took the cartridges out and examined the barrel, noticing that the gun appeared to have been recently fired. He asked when it had last been fired and Richard said, 'last Saturday week' then reloaded the gun and took it back into the house.

That evening, Robert Buckham took the pony and cart to meet his father at the station on his return from work and asked if he had heard about 'it' in London. 'More trouble?' enquired Mr Buckham. 'Mr and Mrs Watson are found in our pond – they have committed suicide in the pond,' said Robert.

Mr Buckham was understandably upset. 'It is a funny thing for them to come and commit suicide in my pond. They might have committed suicide in their own place instead of fetching trouble to me,' he said. Robert said he thought he knew why they had done it. He said their crops were 'upside down' that the potatoes were 'bad', not having grown downwards. He thought Watson had gone to the pond and, finding very little water there, his wife had threatened to leave him.

Only later did Buckham hear that Watson had been shot in the back. 'A man could not shoot himself in the back,' he observed. 'It seems a funny thing.' Later that evening a resident of the neighbourhood passed the spot and, seeing Richard Buckham Jnr there alone, stopped to talk to him. It was just before dark and they commented on the blood, which could still be seen in the area. 'It looks like murder,' said the neighbour. 'It does,' said Richard, casually lighting a cigarette.

In the early hours of the following morning Superintendent Marden went to the Watsons' bungalow. The bodies were still there and he examined them, seeing scattered shot wounds on the back of Mrs Watson's neck, a very large wound

Sergeant Giggins. (Courtesy of the Essex Police Museum)

in the chest and a large wound in her upper arm, which had shredded the muscles. Watson had been shot only once, leaving a large jagged wound, and his right hip was peppered with shot. In the bedroom there was evidence of a search as the bedclothes had been removed from the bed and the contents of a chest of drawers disturbed. A writing desk had also been opened and searched. A desk in the living room was open and in it was an open empty purse. The only money found was two farthings. It was now about 7 a.m. and Marden and Sgt Giggins went to Sawyers Farm and saw Richard and Robert Buckham and their mother.

Marden asked the brothers to show him the spot where they found the bodies, and Richard and Robert took the policemen to the field, pointed out the pond, and then helped the police search the hedgerows for a gun. As Robert assisted Marden, the boy became increasingly agitated and began to cry. Marden, certain that the brothers knew more than they were telling, issued a formal caution and told Robert, 'I believe you and your brother know something about the matter.' He then made a note of Robert's statement.

'I did not do it,' said Robert, 'Dick done it. When he saw them at the pond hole he said to me, "I will shoot them" and pointed the gun at them and fired. I was frightened and went away. I only heard the shots.' A short distance away Richard was helping the sergeant to search and Marden took Robert over to them. He cautioned the brothers and formally charged them both with wilful murder.

'You did it, Dick,' said Richard. 'Tell the truth. I never done it. He wanted me to do it some time ago.' 'I done it in the heat of passion,' said Richard. 'I never meant to do it. I lost my temper. Mr Watson would not go away when I told him he could not have the water... I fired three shots into them. I don't know what made me do it. Bob saw me do it. He was with me.'

The police took both the prisoners back to their house. Richard said, 'I took the door key from Mr Watson's pocket, went to his house and unlocked the door. I didn't go in. Bob was in the lane, waiting.'

Marden remained outside the house in the yard with the two prisoners while Giggins went into the Buckhams' house and brought out the shotgun. 'That is what I done it with' said Richard. The prisoners were taken separately to Billericay police station where both were charged and Richard made an additional statement. 'I wish to tell the whole truth for mother's sake. I did go into Mr Watson's house, and took 4s and 8½d and a silver watch.'

Robert said, 'he showed me the money and the watch when he came out but I did not have any of it.' The brothers were placed under arrest and as the police were taking them away they passed Mr Stevens in Honeypot lane. Robert turned to him and said 'Mr Stevens! Look, Mr Stevens, my brother has done this and they are taking me, as well.'

With the help of Mrs Buckham the police were able to piece together the brothers' movements on the day of the murder. She had got up at a quarter to six and Richard had been up and dressed shortly before. When her husband left for work Richard had already gone out to see to a horse and Robert was just getting up. She made them some tea and at about a quarter past six they went out to shoot rabbits, Richard carrying the gun. 'Don't go out rabbiting this morning,' she said to them, 'dad is so cross if the work is not done.' They took no notice, and she began cooking bloaters for their breakfast. The boys were back in about twenty minutes and sat down to their breakfasts but Robert, usually a hearty eater, had very little and said he felt sick. The brothers went out for an hour to do some general work then returned after an hour for a wash and took the tubs and pails to collect water for the cattle from the pond. After a time, Robert came running up the path crying, 'Oh! Mother, mother! Mr and Mrs Watson are in the pond.' She asked what was the matter and if they were dead, and he said, 'I believe Mrs Watson moved. Dick has run for Mr Stevens.' He wanted a rope but they found some reins and she went running with him to the pond, finding Richard and Mr Stevens there. She saw the bodies, but Richard pushed her away, saying, 'This is too sickening a sight for you,' and Mr Stevens advised her to go back home.

When Robert returned home he said, 'What will dad think? It will be a blow to dad, it being in our pond.' Mrs Buckham prepared dinner for her sons at 1 p.m. Robert still had little appetite but Richard came in and ate his dinner. Both sons said they thought that the police would find that the Watsons' deaths would be a case of murder then suicide. Richard went out, returning later to collect the cart and fetch his father from Laindon station.

That night Richard Jnr was up late with a tooth-ache and Mr Buckham, saying that his sons had had a dreadful shock, suggested to his wife that they be allowed to lie in the next morn-ing, but not too long. Mrs Buckham found young Richard talking in his sleep saying, 'It's all over,' and when he woke he said he

Thomas Stevens.

had had hardly any sleep because of toothache and pains in his head. Richard, she added, had been complaining of headaches for a week past.

On Friday evening the bodies were removed to the Billericay Workhouse Infirmary where the Watsons' younger son, Samuel, identified the remains. On the same evening the brothers appeared before Mr A. Ward JP at Billericay for a formal remand. Richard appeared calm but Robert was in tears.

The post mortem was carried out on Saturday by Home Office expert Dr William Henry Wilcox assisted by Dr Cresswell. He found a hole on the right side of Albert Watson's back an inch and a half in diameter, surrounded by a circle of isolated shot marks 7in across. The right kidney was almost completely destroyed, and there was extensive damage to the liver, aorta and intestines. After carrying out experiments with a breast of mutton, he estimated that the shot had been fired from a distance of 12ft. Mrs Watson had been shot twice. There was an area of gunshot injuries on her head, neck and back measuring about 8 by 5in, and some scattered shot on her right arm. He thought that all these wounds had been made by a single discharge fired from a distance of 18ft. On the front of the body was an elliptical hole over the breastbone about three and a half by two inches and around this were wounds produced by scattered shot. The upper part of the breastbone was destroyed and there were wounds to the ribs, lungs, heart and aorta. To produce these injuries he thought the gun had been fired from about 8ft away. It was obvious that none of the injuries on either of the Watsons could have been self-inflicted. Scratches and grazes on Mrs Watson's body suggested that, after being shot, she had been dragged to the pond hole.

On Sunday 26, thousands of people poured into the area to see the scene of the crime. They travelled by every means available, train, car, motorcycle, carriages, brakes, wagonettes and even on crutches. Never had so many bicycles been seen going up and down Honeypot Lane. The houses of both the Watsons and the Buckhams were stared at from the lane but the main focus of interest was the dank, dark pool where the murder had taken place. There was a cluster of people standing around it in a circle as deep as the surrounding trees, brambles and hedges would allow.

The local newspapers later reported that the pond that lay at the centre of all this fascination was a small, dug-out place almost hidden by hedges and trees. There was very little water in it, and what there was looked dirty and unfit for humans to drink. Part of the bottom was just mud, and on it there remained a large patch of blood on which buzzing flies had settled.

From overheard conversations it was obvious that the crowds had come not only from Essex but London and adjoining counties. Then there were the relic hunters, men who used knives to cut out parts of the bushes in which pieces of shot remained embedded, while others pulled branches from the oak tree overhanging the pond as souvenirs. Cyclists were seen riding away carrying branches on their machines. Some people had arrived with newspapers in which to read about the tragedy, or perhaps to serve as guides to the right spot, and these were later left scattered along the lane.

The Watsons' house was guarded by a police sergeant and a plain-clothes officer, who were posted at the gate of the field in which the bungalow stood. It was possible to see from the road however that the Watsons had kept their smallholding very clean and tidy. The garden was well cultivated with potato and tomato plants and there was a neat stack of hay by the side of the field. The blinds of the bungalow were down and all was silent except for the noise of the chickens and geese, which were being fed by a policeman. At the Buckhams' house all was quiet and still except for the younger daughters who were out feeding the fowls and calves.

That Sunday Samuel Watson went to his parents' bungalow with Sergeant Giggins and searched it to see if anything was missing. The only thing he believed to have been stolen was his father's silver watch, which used to hang on a nail over the bed.

The two prisoners were quiet and well-behaved in their respective cells. They slept soundly at night and sometimes also in the day, but were under constant watch. Robert was more affected and cried a great deal. Each repeatedly enquired about the other. They were given bread and butter and tea for breakfast and at tea time, and at dinner had meat and potatoes with water to drink. On Sunday their mother sent them some apples, which they ate and enjoyed, and each wanted to know if the other had eaten his apples. Messages bidding each other 'good night' were allowed to be taken from cell to cell.

Their next court appearance was on Monday 27 August. The case for the prosecution was conducted by Superintendant Marden, and Captain Showers, the Chief Constable of Essex was in court. Prior to the hearing, Mrs Buckham and an older sister had visited the brothers in the cells, and as the two women left and walked down the street both were crying bitterly.

The brothers both sobbed in court, Robert being the more emotional, but both gradually calmed down and watched the case with a quiet, sorrowful attitude. The slightly built brothers seemed little more than boys; Richard, though nearly twenty-one, had only a light down on his upper lip. After the hearing they were taken back to the cells and from there to Chelmsford Gaol.

Local newspapers observed that the problems of the isolated Essex bungalow dweller had been brought into special prominence by the Basildon tragedy. There was, however, no sign of fear amongst the residents, many of whom didn't bother to fasten their doors at night. A resident of Woodham Ferrers said that burglary in those parts was almost unknown and they never saw tramps, but a Basildon dweller pointed out that the reason why they had no fear of burglars is that they had 'precious little for anyone to steal.'

Mr Stevens, the dairyman, had his own comments to make to the *Essex Herald's* reporter. 'You can do this place a good turn if you urge upon the Billericay Rural Council – firstly the need for a proper water supply, and secondly the need of the hedges being cut in the neighbourhood.'

On Tuesday 28 August, the Watsons were buried at Great Burstead churchyard. Many family and friends and past colleagues of the Watsons came up from London to pay their respects, and mourners spoke movingly of the couple, as honest true and upright Christian people.

At the inquest, held at the Billericay Courthouse, Mrs Buckham gave an account of the morning of 23 August. She was clearly distressed as she told the court her story and a policeman handed her a glass of water. She lifted it to her mouth with a trembling hand and drank deeply before continuing her testimony, in a voice so quiet it could barely be heard. As she completed her evidence, she was convulsed with grief and hid her face in her hands. She left the court, and Robert whispered something to her, but the words were not audible to the press. Richard did not even look at his mother as she passed the dock.

Mr Buckham told the court that both his sons knew of the arrangement for the Watsons to take water from his pond, and that Robert had told him that the Watsons had drawn water for their chickens. He had never withdrawn his permission. Some cartridges were shown to him and he identified them as ones he had bought eighteen months ago. Neither of his sons had permission to use the gun – in fact he had instructed them not to.

Mr Stevens was asked to identify the pails and bath found by the pond hole. The bath was produced in court and contained a large piece of bloodstained turf, which the police had dug from the top of the pond.

The inquest hearing was completed on Friday 31 August. The prisoners, who had been in Chelmsford Gaol, arrived handcuffed together and sobbed in the dock. As Mr Buckham left the court, visibly distressed, Robert murmured, 'Good-bye father.'

Dr Wilcox gave evidence of the post-mortem using a wooden figure representing a human being to point out the position of the wounds. The coroner's jury returned verdicts of wilful murder against Richard Jnr and accessory to murder against Robert.

Scenes in the Basildon magistrates' court.

On 7 September, Robert and Richard Buckham appeared at Billericay Police Court and were committed for trial. Dr Wilcox revealed that the shirts and boots of both brothers were speckled with blood. His testimony was too much for one onlooker, a lad who keeled over in a faint and had to be carried out.

The brothers were given religious books to read, but on 16 October, when a search was made of Richard's cell, it was found that he had been tearing the pictures out of his books and using the unprinted backs to write messages to Robert. The folded papers were discovered hidden under the planks of his bed. The letters gave detailed instructions to Robert as to what to say in court, suggesting that Robert should state in evidence that Mr Watson had thrown a stone at them and then had tried to choke Richard. 'Stick to what you have got because it will be read in court' he instructed, '...this is a serious case... the chaplain said he thinks [I] will get hung if you say I said they drove me mad it will be alright as mother has been ordered to get the copy from the Shadwell Hospital that I was in there with brain trouble.'

The trial took place at the Essex Assizes, Chelmsford on 14 November before Mr Justice J.C. Lawrence. Both prisoners pleaded not guilty in clear and emphatic tones. Mr J. Harvey Murphy for the prosecution suggested that the crime had occurred when Mr Watson was in the pond drawing water, which he intended to hand up to his wife, who was standing on the bank. The first shot was fired at Mrs Watson, who was injured but not killed, and when Mr Watson went to her aid he was shot and died instantly. The person who fired the third shot would have had to reload and then come forward and fire the fatal shot at Mrs Watson. The probable motive was theft as it was thought, although it could not be proved, that the brothers had known that the Watsons had been expecting the delivery of a money order.

The Watsons' funeral procession leaves Billericay.

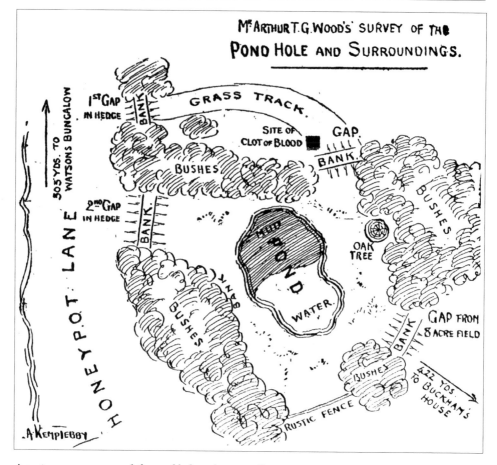

A contemporary survey of the pond hole and surroundings.

The only possible defence was insanity and Mr R. Walker, who defended Richard, questioned Mr Buckham about his family and elicited the information that his grandfather was a hatter who had died insane in a padded cell in Colney Hatch asylum. His mother had had 'a mania for running away and breaking windows' and insulting people and was also 'considered a lunatic.' Buckham said that two of his daughters had 'uncontrollable fits of passion' and Richard had been taken to see a doctor when he was a small child 'because his head was a different shape from an ordinary child's.' The boy had been in Shadwell Hospital when he was seven, had suffered from diphtheria several times and had drooping eyelids. Mr Buckham declared that he did not allow Richard to go out work 'because he is so peculiar and if people were to laugh at him he would be upset and be dangerous.' He had known his son to become dangerous on several occasions, and the least little thing could upset him. Richard Jnr had often complained of headaches and had been unable to work the day before the murder because of this. He worked on the farm where his family could keep him under observation.

Buckham revealed that Richard used to drive him to the railway station in the morning but he had stopped him doing so after an incident in which Richard had jumped out of the back of the gig and left him alone, running away and waving his arms. He did not allow Richard to use firearms as he did not think he was safe with them. Sometimes, when sitting at meals, Richard tore his clothes for no reason. He had also, more seriously, committed acts of cruelty to animals. Buckham had once found Richard cutting up a cat in a chaff machine, and another time he had a cat in a vice and was trying to bore a hole through it. A fortnight before the murder Richard had run at his dog, which had been a favourite, and cut it in half with a shipwright's adze. Afterwards the boy had cried and said he was sorry for what he had done.

Mr Murphy, who had some doubts about the father's claims, questioned Buckham closely, and the witness was obliged to admit that he had never consulted a doctor about Richard's dangerous habits. 'Do you think it is wise or prudent,' asked Murphy, 'for a man, as you say who would cut a dog in two with an adze, to be left in a house where there were children and a loaded gun?' Buckham made no audible reply.

When Mrs Buckham was called to give evidence, she sank down on a chair uttering cries of distress. The prisoners both wept and many people in court, including members of the jury, were seen to wipe tears from their eyes. She confirmed that Richard had had fits and pains in the head and that when he was a baby she had taken him to a doctor because of his strangely shaped head. He would tear his clothes when the headaches came and afterwards be very penitent. Both parents said that the younger son, Robert, was very mild-tempered.

The suggestion that Richard might be insane was not assisted by the revelation of his detailed letters to his brother, which were read out in court. Whether there had been any earlier letters which had reached Robert was not known.

In the witness box, Robert described how he and his brother had gone out to shoot rabbits and when they found the Watsons taking water from the pond Richard had told them not to. He described a quarrel, during which Watson had sworn at the brothers, and then a struggle between Albert Watson and Richard. He had run away to get his sister then heard some shots and came back. Richard, he said, had made him promise not to say what had happened or he would shoot himself. Three weeks previously, his brother had been in a temper about the Watsons taking water from their pond and had said they should stop or he would shoot them. Murphy suggested to Robert that Watson had not sworn at the brothers in front of his wife and that his account of the incident was an invention from papers passed to him by his brother. Robert denied getting any papers from his brother, but his story in court was remarkably similar to that suggested by the letters found in Richard's cell.

'I was afraid of him myself, sir,' admitted Robert. 'Afraid of him?' queried Murphy. 'Well, he had a gun.' Mr Justice Lawrence told the jury that they must decide if the brothers were acting together for a common purpose, in which case both would be guilty of murder. As to the question of insanity, did the jury believe that when Richard pointed the gun at the Watsons and fired, he knew what the result of that action would be and that it was wrong. 'If a man was in a violent passion, one barrel would be enough; two shots would be too much. But to unload the gun, or in this case, load it again and fire a third shot, was something quite different.' The jury had no difficulty in agreeing that Richard had murdered the Watsons, but were divided in opinion as to the state of his mind and his responsibility for his actions. They agreed that Robert was not guilty of murder. The jury retired again and after further discussion returned with a verdict of guilty against Richard.

Richard was sentenced to death, the judge commenting, 'there is nothing whatever in your case to show in the slightest degree that you were irresponsible for your actions.' Mr Murphy did not offer any evidence as to the charge of Robert being an accessory and he was released. He left the court with members of his family and the Salvation Army and was clapped and cheered by the crowds waiting outside.

Unusually, Mr Harry Amos, the foreman of the jury, later made a statement about the deliberations on Richard's sanity. After the first hour the jurors were equally divided, as six of them felt that the prisoner's mental condition meant he could not be responsible for what he had done. After further discussion, the number of jurors who dissented from a verdict of wilful murder was reduced to three. One refused to give in and wanted Amos to tell the judge this but he refused. 'It really looked as if we should have to be shut up for the night, and I began to make preparations for that event. After further deliberation, however, we all agreed.'

Richard spent much of his time in his cell at Chelmsford Prison reading. He ate and slept well and enjoyed a cigarette during his morning and afternoon walk. He was allowed extra fare in the form of a chop for dinner and cocoa for breakfast. On 16 November, his twenty-first birthday, he was told that his execution had been fixed for 8 a.m. on 4 December. He was somewhat surprised at the news but appeared semi-indifferent to his fate. Richard was visited in prison by his mother and an older sister. It was reported that his father and brother were unable to see him due to illness. The congregation of St Mary's Church, Chelmsford, were asked to pray for the condemned man.

The Home Secretary, Mr Herbert Gladstone, received many letters asking him to grant a reprieve to Richard Buckham. The Society for the Abolition of Capital Punishment referred to the evidence of insanity and the prisoner's youth. Many private individuals wrote asking for mercy on the grounds of insanity. Mr and Mrs Buckham also wrote to the Home Secretary, saying, 'we feel sure he could not have been sane when he committed so dreadful a crime.'

A note in the Home Office files dated 20 November stated that the prisoner's previous conduct 'points rather to viciousness and brutality than to insanity' but nevertheless ordered a medical examination by two specialists. Their report on Richard's mental condition stated that, 'Buckham is and was at the time of the murder perfectly sane.' On 30 November the Home Secretary formally denied a reprieve.

What the petitioners for mercy may not have known was that detailed enquiries had been made to check the claims made by Mr Buckham concerning his son's

Chelmsford Gaol.

mental state and fitness for work, and these did not stand up to close examination. Buckham's grandfather had died not from insanity, as he had claimed, but senile dementia, which had only been apparent a few months before his death.

Buckham's statement that Richard was unable to work was also untrue. After leaving school at the age of fourteen, Richard had initially worked for his father, then as an assistant at a fish and chip shop for a year and as a plumber's labourer for a year to eighteen months. During this time, he had shown no signs of insanity, but was considered to be an intelligent, smart lad, and got on well with his workmates. Unfortunately he was also a thief. Richard was discharged by the plumber after stealing order forms from the office and forging one in the firm's name to obtain a lamp, which he then sold. He later stole from his landlady and was turned out of the house, after which he went back to live with his parents. Up to the time of going to Basildon he had been working as a wheelwright. The police interviewed his employers and workmates, who all repudiated the idea that Richard had fits of temper or showed any signs of not being responsible for his actions.

Superintendent Marden made a detailed report on Richard's background, in which he said that he knew the family well and 'so far from the prisoner being in any sense mentally defective or abnormal,' he always regarded him as 'intelligent, sharp and cunning.'

Marden had interviewed Richard Buckham Snr asking him to give proof of his statement about his son's alleged cruelty to animals, but the father was unable to back up his claims. He said that it was only hearsay and he didn't see any of the

Superintendant Alfred Marden. (Courtesy of the Essex Police Museum)

incidents himself. Marden also interviewed neighbours near 475 Old Ford Road, Bow, the Buckhams' previous home. No one there said that Richard was considered insane, but they did express the view that the parents did not exercise proper supervision of their children. Since the Buckhams had been resident at Basildon, Richard had been 'more or less under the observation of the police' and his conduct had been rational. The rest of the family appeared healthy. In October 1905, Richard and his brother had been arrested for stealing bricks and sent to prison for a month.

The police commented that Richard's 'proceedings after the murder show coolness and deliberation' and it was believed that so far from having occurred in a sudden fit, the murder was deliberate and premeditated for the purposes of robbery and that the story of a struggle was a concoction.

On 4 December, at Chelmsford Prison, Richard Buckham had a last cigarette then walked calmly and steadily to his death.

7

MY DARLING GIRL

Highams Park, 1922

On the edge of Epping Forest is a park about a mile long and 500 yards wide, known as the Highams Park. There, the River Ching winds its way north to south through woodland west of a small boating lake, and the banks on either side are heavily shaded by trees and dense bushes.

The evening of Wednesday, 17 May 1922 was dry and fine, when shortly after 8 p.m., with sunset still half an hour away, Edward George Wallis, a sixteen-year-old clerk of Woodford Green, was walking through the park beside the River Ching after tending his father's allotment. A noise on the other side of the river attracted his attention and he saw two men struggling behind a bush. One of the men, noticing Wallis, came towards him and shouted, 'what do you want?' then told him to 'get out of it!' Wallis said nothing and walked away. He had gone about 150 yards towards Chingford Hatch when he saw the man, who was tall and slim, in his twenties and wearing a navy blue suit, leave the bushes together with a young woman and walk rapidly away. The woman was also in navy blue and wore a mauve hat. Wallis watched them until they were out of sight, then decided to investigate. He jumped across the river and walked to a little bridge in the direction of Chingford Hatch, which he thought the couple might have crossed, but seeing nothing he went to take a closer look at the spot where the struggle had taken place. There he encountered Harold Smith, a works manager of Loughton, and his wife, who had been strolling though the park on their way home after attending the Highams Park Picture Palace. The Smiths had heard a moaning noise in the bushes and discovered a middle-aged man lying on his right side, with his head in a holly bush, partly hidden by the leaves, and his feet on the pathway. Smith spoke to the man but got no reply and, thinking he was drunk, was walking away when it occurred to him that the man might be injured and returned. Wallis told Smith about the struggle he had witnessed, and, taking a closer look at the unconscious man, they saw that his head was covered in blood.

Smith and his wife went for help and at the boathouse they found forest keeper William Green. He arranged for a boy with a bicycle to go for the police, and then hurried to the spot. PC Frederick Bolland was on duty at the Highams Park police box when the boy rode up with news of the discovery. Bolland telephoned Richard McCarter, the station sergeant at Chingford police station, and then went to investigate.

McCarter cycled to the scene. A coat had been thrown over the injured man, whose wounds were bleeding profusely, and the sergeant helped to lift him out of the bush. The man was respectably dressed in a dark grey mixture suit and a white collar and dark tie, with a dark overcoat. His light tweed cap lay on the ground nearby. Constable Bolland arrived on foot and was sent to call a doctor. He telephoned Dr Frederick Sanders of 27 The Avenue, Highams Park, telling him to bring some bandages, and returned with a 'hand ambulance'; a wheeled device, not unlike a large perambulator, for transport of the injured.

McCarter could do nothing for the man except bathe his head, but he also searched his pockets for means of identification and discovered a wallet with some trade cards. The injured man was George Stanley Grimshaw, a painter and decorator, of 403 Forest Road, Walthamstow. He appeared to have been the victim of a robbery as there was a piece of broken chain attached to his clothing, which looked as though it belonged to a fob watch. Bolland helped McCarter transfer Grimshaw to the hand ambulance, but when Dr Sanders arrived he told the police that the wounds were very severe and the casualty should be admitted to hospital immediately. Bolland was sent to telephone for a motor ambulance.

Forest Road, Walthamstow.

Police with hand ambulance.

The Highams Park.

It was not until 9.55 p.m., nearly two hours after being attacked, that George Grimshaw was admitted to the receiving ward of Whipps Cross Hospital. He was in a state of acute shock, cold and clammy, almost without a pulse. There were a large number of wounds on the left side of his head, which was 'in a bruised and pulpy condition.' His skull was so badly fractured that in some places it was shattered into small fragments, the bones protruding through his scalp. There were also bruises on both hands and his right arm.

Fifty-four-year-old Grimshaw was a quiet, mild-tempered man, only 5ft 1in tall, with a sallow complexion, light hair and small moustache. He had married Charlotte Ridley in November 1886. The couple had four children, of whom three were married, and in 1922 the Grimshaws and their youngest son, Alfred, were sharing a four- room apartment in Forest Road, for which they paid rent of 13s a week. Grimshaw was a man of routine. He normally came home from his work on the Walthamstow Housing Scheme shortly after 5 p.m. After having his tea he would get some cigarettes and read a newspaper, and then between 7.30 p.m. and 9 p.m. he would go out for a walk and return home at 10 p.m.

On 17 May, however, he had gone out at about 6 p.m., saying that he was going to the dentist to have a fitting for a new set of dentures. He had been accompanied part of the way by his married daughter, Mrs Minnie Austin. At about 6.30 p.m., Grimshaw had called at 252 Hoe Street, Walthamstow, where he had a fitting for his new dentures, but he was there for only a few minutes. After that, his movements were not known. When he was late home, the family became anxious and his son went out looking for him, but soon afterwards, they received the news that he was lying injured in hospital. Minnie Austin and her mother hurried to the bedside of the unconscious man. The only explanation they could offer for his presence in the Highams Park was that he might have been visiting friends in the area. Charlotte was able to confirm that her husband usually carried a fob watch, and he also had a purse which contained between £4 and £6. This was a lot of money to the Grimshaws, and she had told him to bank it but he refused.

In the early hours of the morning of 18 May, George Grimshaw died without having regained consciousness.

Superintendent Wensley of Scotland Yard took charge of the enquiry with Divisional Detective Inspector Tom Tanner of Tottenham. The police issued a description of the murdered man, asking anyone who had seen him after he left the dentist on 17 May to come forward, and also circulated a description of the two people seen running away from the scene of the crime. The Ilford police telephoned to say that the description matched the appearance of a couple who had been sleeping in outbuildings at Highlands Farm. They kept the area under surveillance but the couple had gone and did not return.

Tanner and Wensley visited the scene of the crime, which lay between a path known as 'the Sales' and the River Ching. With one's back to the river the path on the right led to the Dun Cow public house and to the left was the Royal Oak, the murder site being about midway between. They found evidence of a struggle and patches of congealed blood on the ground and spattered on the leaves of the holly bush and adjacent bushes.

The post-mortem was carried out by Bernard (later Sir Bernard) Spilsbury on 20 May. Grimshaw had suffered twenty-six recent bruises and wounds, thirteen of which were on the left side of the head. The coverings of the brain were torn beneath the fractures and the brain itself was bruised and torn. The cause of death was shock and loss of blood. It had been a brutal and callous crime. Spilsbury reported that most of the injuries had been caused when Grimshaw was lying on the ground.

At the inquest, which opened at West Ham Infirmary on 22 May, the eight jurors had gone to view the body when it was realised that Charlotte had not yet made a formal identification. 'This small, sad-faced woman', as the *Walthamstow and Leyton Guardian* described her, had borne herself bravely in court, but sobbed bitterly as she was led out to perform this necessary duty. The enquiry was adjourned to 7 June.

Meanwhile, the area around the crime scene was being carefully searched for any clues that might lead to the killers. On 22 May, a broken umbrella was found about 30 yards south of the holly bushes, and on the following day, William Green was patrolling the bank of the River Ching and found a broken piece of the same umbrella in the water. On 24 May, a heavy spanner about 10in long was found

The discovery of George Grimshaw in the Highams Park and his death in hospital.

The grave of George Stanley Grimshaw, Walthamstow cemetery 2414 D, now taken over by a later burial.

standing almost upright in the stream in a spot where the water was only 6in deep. It was 31 yards from the murder site, and bore traces of what looked like blood.

On the same day, George Grimshaw was buried at Walthamstow cemetery. Charlotte was attended by a St John Ambulance nurse, but after the ceremony she collapsed at the graveside and lay prostrate on the ground surrounded by her family. After receiving treatment she was assisted to the funeral carriage in a state of great distress.

The police were working on the assumption that Grimshaw had been killed in a random attack, when information emerged which suggested that the presence of both victim and murderer in the same location had not been a chance meeting, and that there was more to quiet, inoffensive George Grimshaw than his family realised.

Leonard Hart of Blackhorse Lane, Walthamstow, was a labourer who worked with Grimshaw. On 24 May he made a statement to the police saying that on 17 April, which was Easter Monday, he had gone with his wife and friends to a fair in the forest opposite the Rising Sun public house, and went into one of the cottages near the fair to have tea. In the front room, there were three tables and Grimshaw was sitting at one of them with a young woman. Hart, who may well have felt some embarrassment, said, 'Hallo George, are you round here?' He left shortly afterwards. When he next saw Grimshaw at work, the incident was not mentioned.

On the same day, Detective Sergeant Charles Wesley and Inspector Tanner received the information that broke the case. The informant may have been anonymous as the source was not mentioned in the official report. George Grimshaw had been corresponding with a girl called Mackenzie, who was said to be a waitress in a teashop in Woodgrange Road. The police made enquiries at all the tea shops in the area without finding her, but they learnt that a girl named Elsie Mackenzie had been receiving letters at an accommodation address in Woodgrange Road since August 1921. They called, and found a letter was still there waiting for her.

The letter, postmarked Walthamstow Monday 15 May, was from George Grimshaw asking Elsie to meet him on Tuesday instead of Wednesday and continued:

> Dear you have all to gain I will be alright so cheer up my Darling girl good bye till Tuesday in haste.
> George
> PS I wanted to send a little Postal but can't get away.

Mrs Grimshaw later identified the handwriting as her husband's. She told the police that George, who she described as 'a quiet and reserved man', had gone out on the evening of Tuesday 16 May and returned at 10 p.m. She didn't know where he had been and had had no idea that he had been 'carrying on' with another woman.

At the accommodation address the police learned that in 1921 Elsie had lived at 156 St Paul's Road, Highbury. There they found Mrs Alice Withers, who said that Elsie, whose real surname was Muckle, was her sister. Elsie had been calling herself Mackenzie and had recently married a man called Yeldham at Braintree. Mrs Withers added that Elsie had written asking her to send money.

On 26 May, Superintendent Wensley, Inspector Tanner and Sergeant Wesley drove to Braintree police station and spoke to Superintendent Joyce. Station Sergeant Harry Albert Girt recalled that on 22 May he had seen two people in Braintree who were strangers to the town, answering the description of the wanted couple. He and Wesley were sent to look for them. It was decided that, if found, the couple would be told only that they were wanted for questioning about their recent marriage, which had taken place without the required period of residence.

Girt and Wesley searched the area with an energy and thoroughness which was later highly commended, and at 8.45 p.m. that evening they were at Nunnery Farm in Bocking a village two miles from Braintree, when they saw the tall, slim figure of William Thomas Yeldham standing against some farm buildings. They asked him to come with them to Braintree police station to discuss the marriage. Yeldham introduced a petite young woman as his wife – it was Elsie – and she showed the police her marriage certificate. The couple readily accompanied Girt and Wesley to the station. On the way Yeldham said to Wesley, 'I know what you have got us for, you come from the "smoke" don't you...Where are we going to, are we going to London?' 'I cannot tell you' said Wesley, and Yeldham replied, 'I don't care, I shall be with her wherever we go.' When searched at the station, a tin of rat poison was found on him. Inspector

Tanner interviewed Yeldham first, saying that enquiries were being made into the death of George Grimshaw and that he answered the description of a man seen in the area at the time. Yeldham claimed that on the day of the murder he had been at Highlands Farm, Ilford, where his mother and grandfather lived.

Tanner next questioned Elsie, who said, 'I know all about it, we have seen it in the newspapers; I will tell you all I can.' He cautioned her and she said, 'I only want to tell the truth.' She then made a statement. Elsie gave her name as Elsie Florence Yeldham, formerly Mackenzie, and said that she was a twenty-two-year-old domestic servant living at 55 Albert Road, Braintree. She said she had known Yeldham for nine months. On 17 May they had quarrelled and she told him she was going to see her sister but that wasn't true, she was going to meet Grimshaw. She thought Yeldham must have followed them but she had not been aware of it. She and Grimshaw went to the Highams Park and sat down near some bushes on Grimshaw's coat. At the time she had been wearing a navy costume and a mauve hat and had an old umbrella, which she stuck in the ground nearby. Grimshaw put his arm around her waist and she put hers around his. As they sat there by the river, Grimshaw laid his head on her shoulder, and then, said Elsie, she suddenly saw Yeldham coming up behind them wielding a piece of iron. He struck Grimshaw on the head, and Grimshaw got to his feet but Yeldham kept on hitting him, until the older man fell. Elsie knew that Grimshaw was in the habit of carrying money with him, so she searched him and found the purse, which contained £15 in notes, which she gave to Yeldham. Just then they saw a young man watching from the other side of the river and Yeldham told him to 'clear off.' As they walked away, Yeldham threw the purse into the hedge near the Dun Cow public house. They took a bus to Aldgate and that night slept in a lodging house nearby. The next day Yeldham bought a new suit and boots. He tied up his old things in a parcel, put them in a cloakroom at Liverpool Street Station and tore up the ticket.

When Elsie had finished speaking Tanner went to the charge room to see Yeldham who gave the same Braintree address and said, 'I know what you really want me for.' He was cautioned and made a statement. 'I have done my best for the girl who is now my wife to keep her from the streets' he said. He continued:

> Not long ago she came home wearing a seven guinea costume, and when I questioned her as to where she got it, she said her brother-in-law had given it to her. I was suspicious and learned that she was carrying on with a man, and last Wednesday week I followed her to Highams Park. She met Grimshaw, and I saw them sitting near the holly bush, his head upon her shoulder, and her arm around his waist. She was kissing him. I lost my temper and hit him with the spanner I had. I am sorry, now, I did it in a passion. She has told me since he was a married man.

Tanner told both prisoners they would be taken back to London and charged with murder. They made no reply. Later the same day Tanner and Girt took Yeldham to Stoke Newington police station by car. On the way Yeldham pointed to a road leading to the village of Panfield, saying, 'It was down that road where I sold the watch.'

William and Elsie Yeldham pictured shortly after their arrest.

'Was it in a public house?' asked Girt. 'No,' said Yeldham, 'to a man on a bicycle out-side a little general shop.'

They were passing through Dunmow when Yeldham said, 'I came here last Saturday night and got drunk.' After some reflection he added, 'I am sorry for Mrs Grimshaw but not for him. A married man like him has no right to carry on with a young girl. I put the spanner I did it with in the stream and got in there and washed the blood off my hands.'

Elsie was driven to London by Superintendent Wensley and Sergeant Wesley. On the way she said, 'I've got some of the blood on my costume now, we tried to rub it off when we were on the bus going to Aldgate.' A little later she said, 'I met Mr Grimshaw at 5 to 10 minutes to 7 that night at the Green Man, Leytonstone. We had a cup of tea at the Italian shop just down the road and went to the Woodford Castle by bus, then we went to the back of the Wilfred Laws Inn and sat down near the road at the back. Grimshaw said he didn't like the place and we went to where you found him. He told me he saw a man lurking about.'

They were passing the Rising Sun public house when she said, 'This is where I first met Mr Grimshaw, it was when there was a fair on, I believe it was Easter Monday. He told me he was married, it is a bad job for his wife.'

On 27 May, Edward Wallis identified William Yeldham from a line-up at Stoke Newington police station as the man he had seen struggling with Grimshaw. At another line-up, he identified Elsie as Yeldham's companion. Elsie was shown the umbrella recovered from near the scene of the crime, and said that it was the one she had left there. It was the property of William's mother.

Sergeant Girt had recovered Grimshaw's fob watch that morning. The man on the bicycle was Ernest Laurence, who had bought the watch for 2s and immediately sold it on to Mrs Gowers of the Panfield Arms. Laurence was brought to Stoke Newington and identified William Yeldham as the man who had sold him the watch. Mrs Grimshaw confirmed that the watch was her husband's property.

James Yeldham, William's seventy-six-year-old grandfather, identified the spanner as one he used on the farm. He had last used it on the afternoon of 17 May and then hung it up in the stable. He had seen William go to the stable at about 5.30, and on the following morning discovered that the spanner was missing.

Yeldham's parcel was recovered from the cloakroom at Liverpool Street Station. It contained a blue serge suit, two shirts, a pair of socks with suspenders, a pair of boots, braces and a cap. The right arm of the jacket and front of the legs of the trousers were stained with what looked like blood. Yeldham's mother, Alice, later identified the clothes as her son's property. They and the spanner were taken to Home Office analyst Dr Roche Lynch for the stains to be examined.

Inspector Tanner did not believe that Elsie knew nothing of Yeldham's intentions; neither did he think the motive for the crime was jealousy. He was convinced that the couple had conspired to steal Grimshaw's money and that the plot had already been determined when Yeldham took his grandfather's spanner. Tanner then considered the route that Yeldham was supposed to have taken when following Elsie. From Highlands Farm it was a walk of three quarters of a mile down a quiet suburban road to the nearest bus stop, where buses left every seven minutes to the Green Man. From there it was necessary to catch another bus to Woodford. Tanner thought it very improbable that Yeldham could have followed Elsie from Ilford to the Green Man and changed buses to Woodford, a total distance of 6 miles, without her being aware of it.

At 7.30, Tanner told both prisoners they would both be charged with the wilful murder of George Grimshaw and robbery. They made no reply. The last important discovery was Grimshaw's purse, which was found on 28 May by a police constable searching the bushes in Chingford Lane.

Police enquiries about the couple revealed that both had a record of petty crime. William James Yeldham, born in Hornchurch on 14 November 1899, was the son of an agricultural labourer. He left school at thirteen and worked first as a van boy then as a labourer for his grandfather. In 1915 he joined the navy, signing up for twelve years service as an ordinary seaman. In December 1917 his father, John, died in Brentwood mental hospital from general paralysis of the insane. This was at the time commonly due to syphilis, although his widow believed that it was the result of a head injury he had suffered after a fall at the age of eighteen. Until his father's death, claimed Alice, William had been of good character but thereafter she could only describe his behaviour as 'indifferent to fair.' In May 1919 Yeldham deserted from HMS *Barham*. In June he was briefly in custody in Birmingham on a charge of shop breaking but was discharged. He was finally apprehended and returned to his ship, where he was sentenced to sixty days detention and in September, after serving fifty days, he was dismissed. Since then he had worked for a few months on the roads at Dagenham for his father's cousin, but soon drifted into petty larceny. In February and April 1921 he had been convicted of stealing fowls.

Elsie was born Phoebe Elsie Muckle in Barnet in 1902, the fifth of six children. Her mother had died in 1913 and her father Paul, a policeman, died in 1919. Elsie had worked in domestic service, but more recently had been living off the proceeds of casual prostitution.

When William and Elsie met on 17 September 1921, Elsie told William that she had been 'leading an immoral life' and was 'fed up with it.' He asked her whether if she had anyone to look after her she would try to live 'straight.' He took her home and gave her half his food, letting her in at 10 o'clock at night to sleep. 'Home' was a dairy shed at Highlands Farm, where his mother provided him with two meals a day. On 5 November, when they had had no food for two days, they quarrelled because Elsie said she would rather earn money in the old way.

Yeldham went out and stole a bicycle, but he was soon caught, and served six months in Pentonville Prison. On 12 April 1922, Yeldham returned to Highlands Farm. The day after his release Elsie arrived at the farm saying she had been living with her sister in East Ham. She used to go out every day at 3.30, telling Yeldham she was going to see her sister, and would come back with money, usually about 2s and sometimes as much as 5s, which the couple used to buy food. The source of these funds was never revealed, and Yeldham may have chosen to assume that the money came from Elsie's sister. On 13 May, Elsie returned with a parcel containing a hat and a costume, which she said her brother-in-law had bought her for 7 guineas. She went out on 15 May, saying she intended to pawn the items, but was seen by a policeman at Manor Park trying to sell them in the street. She was taken to the police station but was later released without charge. Soon afterwards she admitted to Yeldham that the story about her brother in law was a lie, and the costume had been bought for her by a man in Walthamstow.

Alice Yeldham was at first unaware that Elsie was living with her son, and sharing the meals he ate in the dairy. By 17 May the couple were desperate for funds. Yeldham asked his mother for money and she gave him sixpence. As he left the dairy Alice saw a woman's hands inside reaching towards a shelf. Elsie and Yeldham were in London on the day after the murder and the following day they took a train to Braintree where, according to newspaper reports, Yeldham had a relative with a different surname, who refused to take them in. This may well have been the person living at 55 Albert Road, the address they had given when arrested. William and Elsie were married on Saturday 20 May at Braintree Register Office. A local postman and a post office clerk were witnesses. When applying for the license, the couple lied about the length of time they had lived in Braintree, but it was later confirmed that the marriage was legal. Their honeymoon was a visit to Great Dunmow, where they visited several public houses. For the next few nights their home was Nunnery Farm, Bocking, which lay just behind a Franciscan convent. There was no house there, just farm buildings in which the occupier, Mr Goodwin, kept pigs.

Elsie Yeldham leaves Stratford Police Court.

The newlyweds slept on straw in a barn, and washed in the river Blackwater. Occupants of cottages in Bradford Street, the backs of which run down to the opposite side of the river, had seen them there for several days and regarded them as a couple of young people who had adopted the simple life. Yeldham was a good swimmer and swam up and down the river several times each day. Elsie also swam using handkerchiefs tied together as a bathing costume, the scantiness of her attire attracting some attention. They bought food at local shops, living on bread, margarine and tinned food.

A representative of the *Essex Chronicle*, who visited Nunnery Farm shortly after the couple's arrest, wrote 'A more lonely place could hardly be found so near to habitations.'

Three days after the wedding their stolen money had run out and Elsie sold her wedding ring to buy food. When arrested they had neither money nor food and had sold every item of value they owned. The prisoners' first court appearance was at Stratford police court on 29 May. Elsie originally appeared dressed in the same dark blue costume she had worn at the time of the murder, probably the only garment she owned. Realising that it would be required as an exhibit, a police matron was sent to buy her another costume and returned with a grey striped outfit. Elsie got changed in the cells and the blue costume was put forward as an exhibit and later handed to Dr Roche Lynch.

The results of Dr Roche Lynch's analysis on 8 June were useful but not conclusive. The stains on both Yeldham's and Elsie's clothing gave reactions suggestive of blood but the amounts were too small to confirm its presence. The spanner, however, tested positive for human blood. The couple were committed to be tried for the murder of George Stanley Grimshaw.

Yeldham was held in Brixton Prison, where he was kept under close observation. On 15 July the senior medical officer of Brixton Prison reported that during his stay Yeldham had been rational and well behaved. He ate and slept well and had gained 18lbs in weight. There was no reason to suppose that he suffered from any mental disease or epilepsy. Similarly, when in Pentonville, there had been nothing in his conduct to suggest insanity. It was concluded that the prisoner was sane and fit to plead.

The trial opened at the Central Criminal Court Old Bailey before Mr Justice Shearman on 19 July, and both prisoners pleaded not guilty. The prosecution case, presented by Mr Percival Clarke, was that the couple had conspired to rob and kill George Grimshaw. Yeldham was represented by Mr A.B. Lucy, but when the trial began it was found that Elsie had no legal representation, and Shearman asked Mr Lucy to defend her as well. Since Yeldham had admitted killing Grimshaw, the best hope of the defence was to persuade the jurors that he had been provoked, and ask for the charge to be reduced to manslaughter. It was also hoped that Yeldham's youth, his obvious love for Elsie, and efforts to stop her living an immoral life would make the prisoner an object of sympathy. Mr Lucy must also have believed that if he could introduce a reasonable doubt that Elsie had any foreknowledge of the crime, then there was a good chance she would be acquitted.

The only witness for the defence was William Yeldham. He claimed that on 17 May Elsie had told him she was going to see her sister and he had decided to go out and steal some chickens and had taken the spanner for that purpose. He had seen Elsie and Grimshaw waiting for a bus and decided to follow them. Finding them in the Highams Park he claimed that he had confronted them face-to-face and demanded, 'What are you doing with my girl?' Yeldham's unlikely story was that Grimshaw had provoked the fight by rushing at him. He described a tussle in which the diminutive Grimshaw had managed to get hold of the spanner and attacked him with it and he had knocked it out of Grimshaw's hand and struck him 'in a fit of passion.'

In Shearman's summing up he advised the jury that even if a man did not intend murder he would be guilty of it if he 'did an act that a reasonable man knew to be dangerous to life, it made no difference whether it was done for vulgar robbery or jealousy.' He thought Yeldham's story of the fight was 'a little difficult to believe' and dismissed the idea of provocation. 'It could hardly be considered provocation to find a man having improper relationships with a woman of this character.' He told the jury that if both had taken an active part in the affair then both were guilty of murder, but if they believed that the woman was not part of a plot to lure Grimshaw than she should be acquitted.

The jury was absent for only twenty minutes and found both the prisoners guilty of murder. The judge asked the jury if they had any recommendation to mercy, but there was no reply and several shook their heads. Mr Justice Shearman donned the black cap and pronounced sentence of death. Yeldham stood upright and said nothing but Elsie, on the verge of collapse, was removed by the wardresses in a half fainting condition.

In Pentonville Prison, Yeldham was allowed to write to Elsie, who was in Holloway, and did so almost every day. The letters were passed to Elsie after being read by the prison authorities, who commented, 'none has had any bearing upon the case. They have merely been protestations of affection.' Elsie was also permitted to write to her husband. Their requests to see each other were denied.

Their appeals were heard at the court of criminal appeal on 21 August before Lord Chief Justice Viscount Hewart, Mr Justice Greer and Mr Justice Swift. It was held that there was 'overwhelming evidence on which the prisoners might be convicted of murder' and both appeals were dismissed. On 22 August, however, Elsie was pardoned and her sentence commuted to life imprisonment.

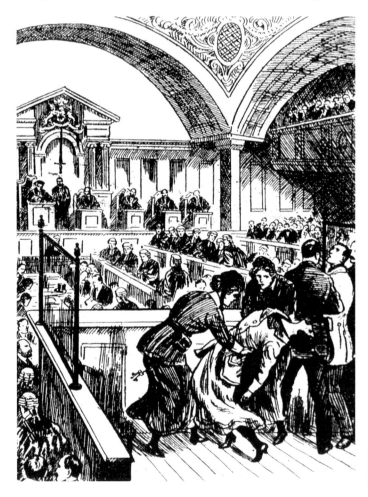

Elsie Yeldham faints in court after being condemned to death.

Yeldham was executed by John Ellis at Pentonville at 9 a.m. on 5 September. The records showed that he was then 5ft 11¼ in height and his weight in clothing was 167lb. Sergeant Girt's zealous and untiring efforts to trace the couple earned him an official reward of £2.

During her time in prison, Elsie received letters from Alice Withers, her brother, sister-in-law and a Mr John Tucker, who campaigned for her early release. Many people sympathised with her, believing that she had been coerced by Yeldham.

Photographs of Elsie taken after her arrest show a young woman with a square face, firm stare, slightly tilted nose and a mop of unruly dark hair. A report dated 6 September said that she was 'of low intelligence, easily influenced and impulsive' but it was felt that she was capable of improvement with careful training. She could do housework and would be able on her release to make a living in domestic service. Elsie, the report observed, was not on good terms with her brother and sister and blamed them for her present position. Nevertheless, her brother was willing to offer her a home on her release.

Elsie was later moved to Aylesbury convict prison, where she was a model prisoner, well behaved, dependable and a good worker. She was freed on licence on 16 July 1931.The pictures taken of her on her discharge show a more relaxed expression and her hair is carefully swept back. She was released into the care of the Aylesbury After-Care Association at the request of its director, Miss Lillian Barker, who had taken a special interest in her rehabilitation.

In 1941, Elsie married and gave birth to a child. She died in 1992 aged eighty-nine.

8

TWO WERE HANGED

Stapleford Abbots, 1927

On the morning of Tuesday, 27 September 1927 William Alec Ward, a Brentwood mail contractor, made his usual collection of mailbags from Romford post office. After delivering bags to Havering and Stapleford Abbots, he drove on in the direction of Stapleford Tawney. Daylight was just breaking, the weather was misty and he drove cautiously though the gloom. At ten minutes to 6 he was going round a bend at Howe Green when his headlights revealed a dark object huddled on the roadside near the hedge. He stopped and recognised Police Constable George Gutteridge, lying half seated against the bank, his legs extended into the roadway. 'Hallo, George, what's the matter?' he asked, but received no reply. He felt the constable's hand, and it was cold. Realising that there was some-thing seriously wrong, he ran to nearby Rose Cottage and informed the occupier, Alfred Perrit, who hurried with him to the scene. John Warren, a bus driver, was passing by on a motorcycle and Ward told him what he had found. Warren, after taking a look at the body, went to Abridge, where he told Constable Bloxham of the discovery and then went to give information at Romford police station. Ward drove to the post office at Stapleford Tawney, where he telephoned the police.

The first police officers to arrive at the scene were PC Albert Bloxham and Detective Inspector John Crockford, who examined the body. Constable Gutteridge had been shot dead. There were two bullet holes in his left cheek, and two more shots had been fired, one into each eye. His helmet and notebook were found beside the body and his pencil was still clutched in his hand. Unfortunately, there was no entry in the notebook for that night. Gutteridge's truncheon, torch and fob watch were in his pockets, but his whistle was hanging out of his pocket on its chain, as if he had just blown it. There was a zig-zag trail of blood across the roadway, with more blood at the start of the trail, and a pool of blood underneath his head. Two revolver bullets were found nearby, one of which was partly embedded in the road.

Scene of the crime. (Courtesy of the Essex Police Museum)

Dr Robert Arnold Woodhouse of South Street, Romford, was called and made an examination at the scene before the body was removed to the coach house of the Royal Oak Hotel, Stapleford Abbots. That afternoon, Detective Chief Inspector James Berrett and Sergeant Harris, of Scotland Yard CID, together with officers of the Epping division of the Essex Police, to which Gutteridge had been attached, carried out a detailed search of the murder site.

George Gutteridge, described by his colleagues as 'a very zealous officer', was born in Norfolk in 1891. He had joined the Essex County Constabulary in 1910, left in 1918 to serve in the army, then rejoined in the following year. He had been stationed in Stapleford Abbots from 1922, and lived with his wife, Rose Annette Emmeline (*née* Savill) and two children, eleven-year-old Muriel and Alfred, who was nearly four at 2, Towneley Cottages. Gutteridge was an efficient although not exceptional constable, and his record was not without the occasional small blemish, once for missing his conference point (a spot where officers on duty met to exchange information) and once for drinking on duty, but he had also been commended by the Chief Constable in 1923 for his perseverance and tact when arresting some youths for stealing horses.

On the morning of his death, Gutteridge had met up with another officer, Constable Sydney James Taylor, at a conference point near Grove House, Howe Green, and reported that all was well. Taylor had checked his watch and it was then 3.25 a.m.

PC Gutteridge. (Courtesy of the Essex Police Museum)

They had parted a few minutes later and Gutteridge headed in the direction of his home, which was not far away. Gertrude, Lady Decies, who owned a tea garden at Stapleford Abbots, told the police that between 3 and 4 a.m. she had heard what sounded like revolver shots, and a car had dashed past. The fact that Gutteridge had been about to make notes while his torch remained in his pocket suggested that another source of light had been available – almost certainly the headlights of a car. There was a tyre mark on the nearside bank, and a car had also been heard driving along Mountnessing Road in the early hours of the morning – avoiding Brentwood High Road, where there was always a policeman on duty.

At 7.15 that morning, a constable found an abandoned car in Foxley Road, North Brixton. It was a four-seater Morris Cowley touring car, registration number TW 6120, which was later identified as the property of Dr Edward Lovell of Shirley, London Road, Billericay, some 14 miles from the scene of Gutteridge's murder. The car had been stolen from Lovell's garage between midnight and 7 a.m. Lovell was telegraphed, and immediately came to Brixton and identified the car as his. It had been unmarked and undamaged when he had last seen it but there were now bloodstains on the offside running board and the nearside front mudguard was bent as if from a recent collision. Some bags of surgical instruments which had been in the car were missing. The police found a spent 455 calibre cartridge case on the floor of the car; a Mark IV, an unusual, obsolete kind not made since 1914.

The police issued a description of the Morris Cowley and Dr Lovell's bags and instruments, and appealed for information from any member of the public who had seen the car or the stolen property on the morning of the crime.

The car was examined for fingerprints, which were compared with those already held on record, Dr Lovell's prints being taken for elimination. The steering wheel was detached and taken to Scotland Yard for closer examination. More than fifty detectives began a systematic search of the Brixton and Camberwell district.

Dr Lovell told the police that he had gone to bed at midnight on the Monday and at 9.15 the next morning discovered that the garage lock was broken and his car was missing. He reported the theft at once. The garage was at the top of a slope and the thieves would have been able to let the car run down the slope by releasing the handbrake, enabling them to remove it without starting the engine near the house. At the bottom of the slope there were signs that the car had become temporarily stuck in some rough road material, and it was believed that it would have taken more than one man to push the car out.

On the day after the murder Gutteridge's body was taken to the mortuary at Romford infirmary. The inquest was opened in the board room on Monday 30 September by the coroner for the southern and western division of Essex, Mr C.E. Lewis. Rose Gutteridge, almost overcome by distress, gave evidence of identification in whispers. The inquest was adjourned to 25 November to allow police to continue their enquiries.

The post-mortem was carried out by Dr Woodhouse. He found four entry wounds; two on the left cheek and two under the eyes, and three exit wounds. One distorted bullet was found in the brain. The two wounds on Gutteridge's left cheek were both surrounded by scorch marks, and Woodhouse later estimated that the gun had been held about 10in away. One of the bullets from the cheek wounds had come out of the opposite cheek, fracturing the jawbone. The second had entered the neck, severing the carotid artery. The first would not have been fatal, but the second would have produced death by haemorrhage in a few minutes. The other two wounds were almost symmetrically placed, one below each eyeball. It was Woodhouse's opinion that these two shots had been fired after the other two, while Gutteridge was lying on his back and from only a few inches away. The cartridge case found in the car

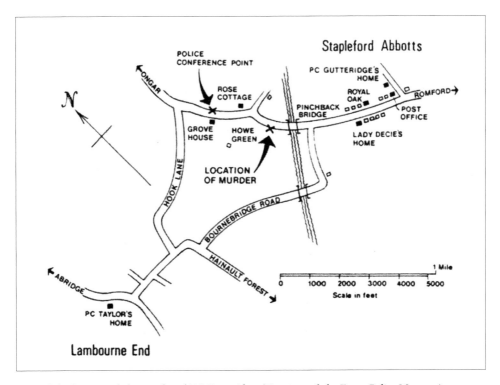

Map of the location of the murder of PC Gutteridge. (Courtesy of the Essex Police Museum)

The murder of PC Gutteridge.

and the bullets found at the scene and removed at post-mortem were given to ballistics expert Robert Churchill, who established that the murder weapon was a Webley revolver.

Gutteridge was buried at Warley Cemetery, Brentwood, on Saturday 1 October. Over 200 policemen including Captain D.A. Unett, the Chief Constable of Essex, were present. Large crowds lined the route and the Bishop of Barking made an address expressing the public admiration for and respect 'to a force to which they owed so much, and which the dead man adorned, not only with his death, but with his life.'

Expectation of a quick arrest remained high, but almost two months later, when the adjourned inquest was resumed, the identity of the murderers was still a mystery, although the police were sure that whoever had stolen Dr Lovell's car had also murdered PC Gutteridge. It was thought that Gutteridge had been about to take particulars of the car's occupants when he was shot, and staggered backwards, leaving the blood trail across the road, then collapsed by the bank. The *News of the World* offered a reward of £1,000, which was later increased to £2,000, but no-one came forward. The coroner's jury, after finding a verdict of murder by person or persons unknown, advised that there should be a telephone in every local constable's house and expressed astonishment that the mail van had been in the charge of only one man.

With no clues leading directly to the perpetrators, the police made a list of known villains, men with records of car theft, who carried firearms. A prominent suspect was Frederick Guy Browne, a thickset, dark-browed man with a number of criminal convictions to his name and a fondness for guns. While he had the skills to earn an honest living, he was rebellious by nature, with a strong antipathy to discipline and authority.

There has long been some confusion about his name and origins. 'Frederic Guy Christopher Brown' (the spelling on his birth certificate) was born on 10 February 1882, the son of artist Frederick Murray von Kalckreuth Brown. Frederick later said that he thought he was born around 1881, which may be why, on his marriage to domestic servant Caroline Barson on 4 September 1915, the certificate records his age as thirty-four when he was actually thirty-three. His brother-in-law, Arthur Finch, who had married Frederick's sister Ida in 1913, later claimed that Browne's real name was Leo Brown, and indeed Frederick did have a brother of that name, who appears in the 1891 census aged 1 under the name Leo K. Brown. Finch later sent a postcard to the authorities with a picture of a serviceman, printed with the words 'Leo K. Brown, the real "Mr Browne" who had nothing to do with the death of PC Gutteridge. Scotland Yard calls him "Frederick Guy Browne".'

It is known that 'Leo Brown' recorded as aged twenty in the 1911 census, lived in Eynsham, Oxfordshire with his widowed mother, where, with a brother who was not named by the press, he operated a bicycle repair business. From 1911 to 1913 Leo was convicted on numerous occasions for offences such as petty theft and burglary, and was found in possession of a loaded revolver. The newspaper reports of his trials give an age suggesting that he was born in 1890 or 1891, which makes him Frederick's younger brother, yet it has always been officially believed that the man who was twenty in the 1911 census was the same man who gave his age as thirty-four on his marriage in 1915. A report in the files of the Metropolitan Police, now held by the National Archives, attributes Leo's petty crimes in Oxfordshire to Frederick, but also states that he had a younger brother who went to America. However, while Frederick signed official letters F.G. Browne, his personal correspondence was under the name 'Leo'. If the Frederick Browne suspected by the police really was Frederick the older brother (and the 1927 suspect was the man who married Caroline in 1915), and Leo had gone to America, could Frederick have adopted his brother's name, perhaps as a smokescreen to conceal criminal activities more serious than Leo's?

Whatever his real name, Caroline Browne said that Frederick had always been a good husband to her. He was faithful, neither smoked nor drank, and worked hard to support her and their daughter, Doris, who was born in 1917.

Browne served in the Royal Engineers from 1916 to 1918 and was discharged after being sentenced to ten months' hard labour at Petersfield for stealing a motorcycle. After his release he worked in a garage in Clapham, then moved to Eastwood near Southend, where he stole and altered cars and made fraudulent insurance claims. In February 1923 he, Caroline, Arthur Finch and an associate, career criminal Aubrey Martin, who had been convicted of petty crimes carried out with Leo in Oxfordshire, were all tried at the Old Bailey for conspiracy to defraud and forgery. Browne got four years with hard labour. In Parkhurst Gaol, Browne was a difficult prisoner, refusing to work, damaging his cell and assaulting warders. He was transferred to the harsher regime of Dartmoor, and there he met William Henry Kennedy.

Kennedy, born about 1891, was the son of an Irish mining engineer. After leaving school he trained as a compositor and worked in a newspaper office in Liverpool. He soon took to petty crime and a string of convictions followed; for drunkenness, indecent exposure and house breaking. There were also periods of military service. In 1924 he stole a bicycle when carrying a loaded revolver and received a sentence of three years, part of which he served in Dartmoor, where he met Browne. He was released in November 1926.

Browne was discharged from prison in March 1927, and decided to set up another car repair business. In June he found a yard and lean-to shed at 7a Northcote Road, and began to convert it into a garage, suitable not only for legitimate work, but as a cover for criminal activities. The completed premises, known as the Globe Garage, included an inner office with a bed where staff could stay overnight, and Browne slept there while he was getting it fitted out. Caroline was working as a cook/housekeeper for a local family. Late in August the family took furnished accommodation and from 24 September they rented a flat at 33a Sisters Avenue. Browne, sometimes with accomplices, was carrying out burglaries and also stole cars, which were brought back to his garage, altered and sold.

Kennedy and Browne must have kept in touch, for according to Kennedy he was working on a farm in Cheshire when he received a letter from Browne, asking him to come down to London and manage his garage. The two men worked together and jointly carried out a number of robberies until 17 December 1927, when Kennedy left.

Inspector Berrett suspected that Browne could be involved in the murder of PC Gutteridge. In January 1928 a stolen Vauxhall car was traced to Browne's garage, which was placed under police surveillance. Browne was in the West Country at the time, meeting a former prison associate who had just been released from Dartmoor. On 20 January, Browne returned to the garage, and was arrested on suspicion of stealing the Vauxhall. In his waistcoat pockets, the police found a driving licence in the name of Frederick Harris, which Browne described as 'the "dud" in case I am stopped', a set of skeleton keys and a pair of artery forceps. Asked where he had obtained the forceps, he claimed that he couldn't remember. In his coat pocket was a stocking mask, and in the back pocket of his trousers were twelve 455 cartridges, one of which was a Mark IV. 'That's done it,' said Browne. 'Now you've found them, it's all up with me.' Constable Frank Bevis searched Browne's car and found a Webley revolver in the pocket next to the driver's seat loaded with Mark IV cartridges. With safety in mind, he unloaded the gun, took it into the garage where Browne was being questioned, and showed it and the cartridges to the police inspectors present. 'You have found that, have you?' said Browne. 'I am done for now.'

The monument to PC Gutteridge.

More cartridges and medical supplies were found in the office. That night the police went to the Brownes' rented apartments at 33a Sisters Avenue and found two loaded guns and more Mark IV ammunition, an ear speculum, which had been adapted to make an inspection light, and bandages. Questioned at Tooting police station, Browne said, 'if you had stopped me when I was in the car I should have shot five of you and saved the other one for myself', adding, '... I shall have to have a machine gun for you b*****ds next time.'

Chief Inspector Berrett told Browne he was making enquiries into the murder of PC Gutteridge and asked him to account for his movements on the night of 26 September and the following morning. Browne remained calm and, after being cautioned, he made a statement, admitting that he was familiar with South Essex, although he denied that he had ever been to Stapleford Abbots. He claimed to have bought the Webley from a sailor at Tilbury docks but said he had never fired it. The gun had begun to go rusty after he bought it and he had had to keep it oiled. He had gone armed, he said, ever since he had been robbed while delivering cars to the country. Most of the medical supplies had been bought at a chemists and the ear speculum at a street market.

Further searches of the garage premises uncovered items which linked Browne to recent burglaries and Bevis found a second Webley in a compartment behind the driver's seat of Browne's car. The second Webley was fully loaded, two of the cartridges being a rare Mark I type. On 23 January Browne was charged with the theft of the Vauxhall. The police were sure that if Browne had murdered Gutteridge he had not acted alone, and were anxious to trace any associates. An informant mentioned Kennedy, who had returned to London on 14 January and had been lodging in Wandsworth at an address which Browne had briefly occupied the previous September, paying a month's rent in advance. On 21 January, Kennedy had received a telegram advising him that his sister was seriously ill, and he and his wife left at once. It was later discovered that Kennedy had visited the Globe Garage that day, seen detectives outside, and had sent the telegram to himself to supply an excuse for his rapid departure. That evening the Kennedys hired a car to take them and their luggage to Euston Station, and boarded the midnight train to Liverpool.

It was not difficult to follow their trail, and the Liverpool police were alerted and kept watch on Kennedy's known haunts. On the night of 25 January, Kennedy, suspicious that the police were surrounding his lodgings, an address he had used before, quickly threw on some clothes, put his automatic pistol in his pocket and fled alone. He was seen and recognised by Detective Sergeant William Mattinson. 'Hallo, Bill, come on,' said Mattinson. Kennedy turned and drew his gun. 'Stand back, Bill or I'll shoot you,' he said. Mattinson tried to take hold of him, and Kennedy pressed the muzzle of the gun into the policeman's ribs and pulled the trigger. There was a click, but no shot. Mattinson twisted the gun hand up with his left hand and punched Kennedy with his right. Kennedy fell, and Mattinson was able to gain possession of the gun, and take his man prisoner before the other officers in the vicinity arrived on the scene. The sergeant had had a lucky escape. There was a live round in the gun, but the safety catch was on. Kennedy was arrested and charged with being concerned with Browne in the theft of the Vauxhall car, but suspecting that he was wanted for a more serious crime, hinted as much to his wife.

The following afternoon Kennedy and his wife were on the train back to London. Berrett and Harris were waiting for him at Scotland Yard, where he was told that he had been detained on a charge of stealing the car but they wanted to know if he could tell them anything about the murder of PC Gutteridge. 'I may be able to tell you something,' said Kennedy, 'but let me consider awhile.' He spent some time deep in thought then he asked to see his wife. Mrs Kennedy was brought into the room and he told her about the enquiries into the murder of Gutteridge. 'Why, you didn't murder him, did you?' she said. 'No I didn't,' said Kennedy, 'but I was there and I know who did.' His next words revealed the options that had been revolving in his mind. Kennedy told his wife that if he was found guilty of murder he would hang but if found guilty of being an accessory after the fact then he would be in prison a long time. 'Will you wait for me?' he asked. She said she would and advised him to tell the truth.

The arrest of William Kennedy.

Kennedy, taking his time and giving his words a great deal of thought, then made a lengthy statement that took almost four hours to record. From time to time he stopped and asked for parts to be read over to him, and he made corrections.

The substance of Kennedy's statement was this: from June or July 1927 he had been working for Browne at the Globe Garage, sleeping on the premises. On 26 September, he had gone out with Browne to steal a Raleigh car in Billericay, not far from the station. They went by train from Liverpool Street shortly after 7 p.m., a journey of just over half an hour. Browne had opened the garage door with a key and they waited in the grounds of the house until the owners went to bed. They approached the house at 11 p.m. but a dog started to bark and they gave up the attempt. They walked on through the village and, spotting Dr Lovell's garage, decided to wait until the lights in the house went out. It was then about midnight. Browne forced the garage door and checked that the car had plenty of petrol in the tank. The car rolled down the slope to the road under its own weight and the two men pushed it about another hundred yards. They then started the engine and drove it around the country lanes, avoiding the main roads. According to Kennedy, Browne was driving and he was in the passenger seat.

On the way to Ongar they saw someone flash a lamp and then a police whistle blew. Browne stopped and the car was approached by a policeman. The policeman asked Browne if he had a licence and Browne admitted he had not. When asked where he came from, Browne stammered awkwardly in his answer and the policeman asked if the car was his. Kennedy said, 'No the car is mine.' The policeman flashed his lamp in their faces, and asked Kennedy if he knew the number of the car. Browne said, 'You'll see it on the front of the car.' By now the constable was clearly suspicious that the car was stolen and said, 'I know the number, but do you?' Kennedy was able to give the car number but the policeman pulled out his notebook and was about to write a report when there were two explosions and Kennedy saw him stagger back. 'What have you done?' said Kennedy, and saw that Browne had a Webley revolver in his hand. 'Get out quick,' said Browne. They both got out of the car and Kennedy went to look at the policeman, who was lying on the ground groaning. 'I'll finish the bugger,' said Browne. 'For God's sake,' said Kennedy, 'don't shoot any more, the man's dying.' Gutteridge's eyes were open and Browne, saying, 'what are you looking at me like that for,' stooped down and shot him at close range through both eyes. They got back in the car and Browne handed Kennedy the revolver and told him to reload it. Kennedy did so, but in his excitement dropped a cartridge case on the floor of the car as it hurtled along at what seemed to him like a great speed. He threw the other three cartridge cases out of the window and handed the gun back to Browne. It was foggy and Browne drove into a tree, damaging the nearside front wing of the car. Browne wanted to drive to the Globe Garage but Kennedy persuaded him not to and they abandoned the car, taking the cases of medical instruments and returning by tram. Kennedy was rattled; he wanted to leave London, but Brown, adamant there was no danger, threatened to blow Kennedy's brains out if he tried

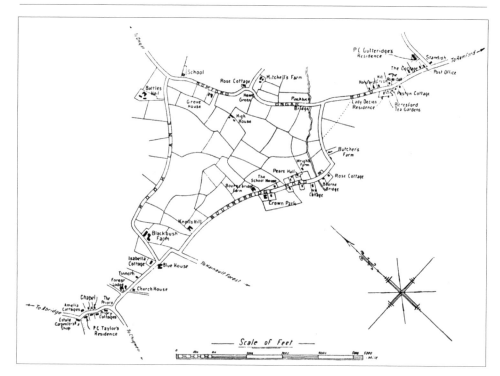

Plan of the neighbourhood of the murder.

to leave. 'You'll stop here and face it out with me,' said Browne. 'If anyone comes here there will be a shooting match.'

In December, however, when Kennedy again said he wanted to leave, Browne raised no objection.

Kennedy's detailed information clearly demonstrated that he was involved in the crime, but Browne had denied all involvement so the police needed to find something other than the statement of a criminal to link him to the murder. The obvious link was the gun. Robert Churchill was able to exclude Kennedy's automatic and two of Browne's guns – the ones found in his flat – from suspicion and was left with the two Webley revolvers, both of which had been found in Browne's car. Churchill and three other experts carried out a number of test firings. Churchill compared the wounds under Gutteridge's eyes with those on the cheek and saw that there was a tattooing around the eye wounds probably caused by black gunpowder. This effect was absent from the cheek wounds and he concluded that the two sets of wounds were caused by different kinds of ammunition. The two bullets found embedded in the ground were Mark I, an even rarer type than Mark IV. Two of the cartridges found in the older Webley were Mark I.

Microscopic examination of the first Webley found, later described in court as exhibit 17, showed a small defect unique to that gun, which had left a distinctive mark on the cartridge case (exhibit 9) found in the doctor's car. There could be no doubt that exhibit 9 had been fired from exhibit 17. Two bullets had been found at the scene, exhibits 7 and 8, and it was found that they were different kinds of ammunition; one was black powder, and one cordite. The bullet removed from Gutteridge's brain was probably a cordite cartridge. Black powder cartridges were an old type that were being phased out and were relatively rare. A live cartridge of this kind was found in the second Webley.

Dr Lovell was brought to Tooting police station to examine the medical instruments. A cautious man, he was unwilling to positively identify the items as his, pointing out that they were of standard manufacture, however they did match the description of the items stolen from his car.

Browne and Kennedy made their first court appearance at the south western police court on 13 February. The charge of stealing the Vauxhall had been dropped and only the murder charge was before the court. When the hearing was resumed on 21 February, the defence did everything possible to attack the validity of Kennedy's statement to prevent it being admitted in evidence. It was claimed that Kennedy had been threatened, that he had been promised that he had nothing to fear as he had been led astray by Browne, that the police had played on his feelings for his wife and that Berrett, together with Superintendent Percy Savage, had subjected Kennedy to a gruelling interrogation. Berrett firmly denied all the imputations, and the chairman of the magistrates, Mr John Brown Sandbach, declared that the allegations made about Inspector Berrett were 'particularly amazing' to anyone who knew him. Kennedy's statement was held to be admissible, and when it was read out, Browne jumped up and exclaimed, 'I hope you are satisfied with the useful way in which the case has been concocted and put together by the police and everybody.' He was ordered to be quiet and sat down with a smile.

Both men were committed for trial, which opened at the Central Criminal Court Old Bailey on 23 April. The prisoners pleaded not guilty. Counsel for both Browne and Kennedy made a request for the two to be tried separately, but Solicitor General Sir Boyd Merriman, prosecuting, opposed the application, saying that the case for the Crown was that the men were 'commonly engaged together on a joint purpose' and Mr Justice Avory refused the application. Merriman told the jury that the statement made by Kennedy was not to be taken as evidence against Browne. The case for the Crown was that Gutteridge had been shot by one or both of the men. They were engaged in a common purpose and therefore both were equally guilty. Kennedy, he said, had, according to his own statement, seen his companion cold bloodedly shoot a man but was prepared to reload the gun and hand it back to him.

Frank Powell opened his defence of Kennedy with the suggestion that Kennedy had not known that Browne was armed that night and could not therefore have colluded in the murder. Given Browne's past record, and the fact that the two men knew each other well, the jury was unlikely to be convinced that anyone with a criminal past who went out on a robbery with Browne would not have suspected he might be armed. Powell did not choose to put Kennedy in the witness box.

Browne however did step into the witness box, where he did himself no favours by querying the words of the oath he was expected to take on the grounds that he could not know 'the whole truth.' He eventually took the oath, explaining that he could only tell the truth as he knew it. He claimed that on the night of 26 September he had not left London. The Webley revolvers were normally kept in the back room of the garage premises where Kennedy slept. They hung on nails on the wall, covered by a coat. Browne became agitated when he said that Kennedy's statement was 'a fairy story from beginning to end' and 'a concoction' and had to be calmed by his counsel, Mr E.F. Lever. Browne told the court that Kennedy was a persistent drunkard and he had often threatened to sack him. He explained his comments about being 'done for' by saying he believed he was in trouble for not having a licence for the gun or ammunition. Powell had claimed in Kennedy's defence that his client was unable to drive a car but Browne declared that Kennedy could and he had seen him do so. 'I put it to you,' said Powell, 'that he has never driven a car at all.' 'You can put it to me,' said Browne. 'I put it to you, why does he take a driver's licence out? People do not take a licence out to drive wheelbarrows.' He suggested that the other man in the car had been 'Kennedy's confederate, the man he goes boozing with, whoever he is.' Powell was later obliged to admit that he had been mistaken in believing that Kennedy had never had a driving licence.

One of the biggest sources of confusion during the trial, and a major plank of the case made by Christopher Berry-Dee and Robin Odell for Browne's innocence in *The Long Drop: Two Were Hanged - One Was Innocent*, is the difference between Browne's original statement to the police regarding the two Webley revolvers and his evidence in court.

The first Webley to be found, which was in a pocket near the driver's seat, was the one later referred to in court as exhibit 17 and shown to be the murder weapon. It was the newer of the two guns and had an oxidised finish so it had not rusted. The second gun was an older model and had started to rust after Browne got it. He had had to keep it oiled. This was exhibit 31.

When Browne was first questioned, only one gun (exhibit 17, the murder weapon) had been discovered, and he told the police that he had owned it since April, and

WEBLEY REVOLVER
found fully loaded by
P.C. Bevis, Met. Police
in Browne's car at
Clapham Junction,
21st January, 1928.

Exhibit 17, the murder weapon. (Courtesy of the Essex Police Museum)

described it as rusty. While someone might lie about the origins of a weapon, it clearly makes no sense to lie about its appearance, which suggests that he may not have got a good look at it and thought that the gun discovered first was the older one. It is noticeable that in Browne's statement about other items such as tweezers and bandages he stated that he had been shown them, but when he referred to the gun he said only that he has been asked about it. When questioned at the trial, he was adamant that it was the older gun, the one that had rusted (exhibit 31), which he had owned since April. At first he refused to say where he had got the newer gun but eventually admitted that he had got it from Kennedy after swapping it with the automatic. The automatic was part of the proceeds of a burglary which had taken place on 7 October, ten days after the murder. At the time of the murder, therefore, according to Browne, the murder weapon was in the possession of Kennedy. Both Webleys had been kept in the garage, but it seems reasonable to assume that had the men gone out together on 26 September each would have carried his own gun, and had Kennedy gone out with another man, he would have been carrying the new Webley. In his statement to the police however, Kennedy said that Browne had carried the newer gun on 26 September.

In court, it appeared as if Browne had changed his story, but it is very possible that when first questioned he was under the impression that he was being asked about the older gun. Browne recognised the crucial importance of the exchange of guns, and tried to smuggle a note out of prison to find out the date of the swap. His wife had visited him in prison on 10 April, and he had written something in invisible ink on the back of a letter she was going to send to Mabel Currie, an eleven-year-old girl. (The police speculated that the 'ink' used was actually urine.) Mabel's father, Charles, had been an associate of Browne and Kennedy in the burglary in which the automatic had been acquired. The message was 'Will you let me know by return the date it was when I exchanged revolvers with Kennedy after he may have shot the PC? Just quote date by return as near as possible.' The letter was intercepted and when the details emerged in court it was interpreted as an attempt by Browne to shift the blame from himself to Kennedy.

The stolen car.
(Courtesy of
the Essex Police
Museum)

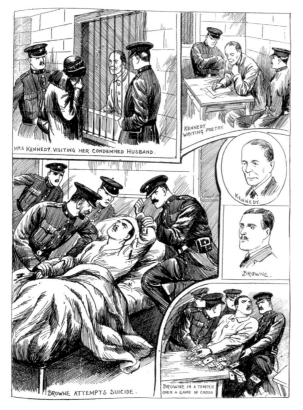

Browne and Kennedy in prison,
May 1928.

One aspect of the case was never questioned at the trial. It was assumed that the first shots had been fired by the driver of the car. At the police court Dr Woodhouse had been asked how easy it would be to fire the shots at Gutteridge if he was standing close to the lamp on the offside of the car. Woodhouse thought it would be difficult for the driver and even harder for the passenger. According to Kennedy, however, the policeman was standing by the running board and had just been questioning the men, which suggests that he was by the window.

The police believed that Kennedy's statement was basically true except that it was Kennedy who had fired the gun. There was nothing to stop the gun being fired from the passenger seat, indeed, given that the Webley had approximately a 6in barrel and the shots in Gutteridge's cheek had been fired from about 10in away while the policeman was standing by the running board, this is a more convincing scenario than the driver being the shooter. Berrett, in his memoirs, stated, 'In my own reconstruction of the murder I place Kennedy as the man who shot first, for I have difficulty in visualising how the driver of the car – admittedly Browne – could have shot from the driving seat not only so that the bullets entered where they did, but could have shot unseen by Gutteridge.' He added that he felt sure that it was Browne who delivered the last two shots. Kennedy, he said, was 'weak-willed, ready to tell all he knew in an effort to save his skin.'

On the last day of the trial, Kennedy volunteered to make a statement from the dock. He declared that his marathon statement to Inspector Berrett was 'absolutely true' and that on the night of the murder he had no idea that Browne was carrying a revolver. He claimed that he had reloaded it because he was terrified and didn't know what he was doing. In his final address to the jury, Lever referred to Kennedy as a 'caged rat', his statement largely composed of lies to save himself.

Mr Powell maintained, unconvincingly, that Kennedy had not known that Browne had a gun, and that he was 'terrorized by the terrible things he had seen and heard.' Browne's statement following his arrest on 20 January, in which he admitted to owning a Webley revolver since the previous April told heavily against him in Mr Justice Avory's summing up, despite the fact that he had very clearly been referring to the rusty revolver that was not the murder weapon.

The jury retired at 12.52 p.m., taking with them a number of exhibits. They returned at 3.10 p.m. and announced that they had found both the prisoners guilty. Browne then made an extraordinary announcement. He acknowledged that the jury had been fair but they 'had stuff given to them which is not genuine.' He was sure it would come out that he had nothing to do with it, but would not try to prove his case as 'there is something hanging over my head so that, if I got off all this, I should get penal servitude for something else, which is far worse than this is for me.'

The failure of Browne and Kennedy's appeals.

The execution of Browne and Kennedy.

He added, 'I am quite content. My conscience is clear.' Kennedy, stating that the verdict was 'fate', declared that he was not afraid to die.

In the early hours of the morning of Saturday, 28 April Browne, who was confined to the condemned cell of Pentonville Prison, attempted to commit suicide by cutting his left arm and leg with a small piece of safety razor. He was stopped by warders and suffered no serious injury.

Both prisoners lodged appeals which were dismissed on 22 May. They were executed on 31 May, Browne at Pentonville and Kennedy at Wandsworth. It is probable that at least two men were involved in the killing of PC Gutteridge, as one man alone could not have pushed the car. Kennedy was undoubtedly guilty, but given that his statement was not evidence against Browne, the case against Browne consists of the following: his possession of the murder weapon, which he may not have owned at the time of the murder, his possession of some of the items stolen from the car, not in themselves positively identified, his past record, which would have been inadmissible in court, and his knowledge of the Essex villages. Flimsy evidence on which to hang a man.

9

THE DUTCH GIRL

Aldham, 1958

On 7 December 1957, nineteen-year-old Mary Kriek from Voorburg in the Netherlands, arrived in Britain to work as a 'mother's helper' at Bullbanks Farm, Eight Ash Green, near Aldham, on the Halstead road, about 3 miles west of central Colchester. The road which passes though Earls Colne on its way to Halstead is flanked on either side by farmland. Large, well-kept farmhouses and outbuildings are sometimes grouped three or four to a row but usually stand alone, widely spaced with fields in between, but are never so far apart that some habitation is not always in view. Mary's employers were Eric and Kathleen French whose two children were nine-year-old James and six-year-old Phillip. Mary was fond of the children and used to walk down to the village shops with them, where, because of her lack of English skills, she appeared very quiet and reserved. 'A pleasant girl, but very difficult to understand,' said a shop keeper at Eight Ash Green, and a friend of the French family said, 'You had to talk to her as a child.'

Mary was an intelligent girl who had attended high school, and, after briefly working in an office, had decided to improve her career prospects by studying languages. She had spent some time in France before coming to England, where in addition to her duties as a nanny she attended classes at Colchester College. Mary had a pleasant, friendly manner, was responsible and well-behaved, and the family quickly grew to like her. 'A very sweet and sensible child,' said a friend of the French family. As Mrs French was to comment, she was 'not a particularly pretty girl.' A picture taken of her in Colchester just before Christmas shows a broad, plain face with a happy, slightly toothy smile, framed by wavy light brown hair. She did not, as far as anyone knew, have any boyfriends.

Mary's sister, twenty-one-year-old Wilhelmina, known as 'Willy', had, until a year earlier, worked as a nanny for South-African born Roger St Clair Fearon and his wife Elizabeth, who, with their three children, occupied Pear Tree Hall Farm,

Mary Kriek. (By kind permission of Newsquest Essex)

Earls Colne. Willy, knowing that Mary wanted to come to England, had recommended her to Eric and Kathleen French.

In December, Mary attended a Christmas party at Colchester Technical College, where she met nineteen-year-old Munich-born Renate Krummeck, who was employed as a mother's help by an American family Mrs and Mrs Faaborg of 'Sesame', Coggeshall Road, Earls Colne. The girls quickly became friends and Renate was invited to tea with Mary at Aldham. When Mary was given the weekend off the two girls decided to go on a trip to London together, and on Saturday 4 January they caught the 1.40 p.m. bus into Colchester, where they took a train into London Liverpool Street. They spent a happy time sightseeing and stayed overnight at Netherlands House. The girls returned to Colchester on the train, and caught the last Halstead bus, the number 88, at 10.30 p.m., which went up the Halstead road, passing Aldham and going on to Earls Colne. In 2010 the last number 88 bus leaves Colchester bus station at 10.40 p.m. and arrives at Eight Ash Green at 10.56 p.m. and Earls Colne eighteen minutes later, and in 1958 the timings could have been little different. The night of Sunday 5 January was fine with a full moon and a clear sky. There was an animated conversation on the bus as the girls talked excitedly about the places they had seen, which included Buckingham Palace, the Tower of London and the Houses of Parliament. Mrs French had retired to bed early and although she heard the bus pass the farm she was too sleepy to be aware of whether or not she had heard Mary come in. The following morning she found that Mary's bed had not been slept in. Thinking that Mary might have stayed overnight in London with Renate, Kathleen telephoned the Faaborgs and discovered that Renate had returned at the expected time on Sunday night and was surprised to learn that Mary was not home. Mary, she said, had alighted from the bus in Halstead Road, and had smiled and waved as the bus moved off.

At 6.45 a.m. that morning Les Peck, of Hill Farm, Langham, who was employed as a tractor driver at Rivers Hall Farm, Boxstead, some 12 miles from where Mary had last been seen, was cycling to work through heavy rain, down lonely Dedham Road, leading from Boxstead Cross Inn to the crest of Dedham Gun Hill, when he saw something white glistening in the light of his cycle lamp. He stopped to investigate and found that it was the shimmer of nylon on the legs of a young woman. She was fully clothed and face down in a ditch, her legs protruding over the brow of the ditch into the road, lying, he said later, 'very tidy like.' 'Are you alright?' he shouted, but there was no reply. He rode on to Rivers Hall Farm, where he reported his find to the bailiff, Ernest Walter Baalham. They returned to the spot in the bailiff's jeep and by the light of the headlamps could clearly see that the girl was dead. The men were careful to touch nothing and drove to Plumbs Farm Langham, the home of a Mr L. A. Allen to telephone the police.

Returning to the spot, they found Mr J Harries a maintenance man at Rivers Hall Farm, who had been cycling a short distance behind Peck, and had stopped to stand guard over the body. Harries had noticed that the girl's shoes were clean. 'She lay there as if she had been laid out' he later told reporters. He also noticed that there were no skid marks near the scene and no signs that there had been either a struggle or an accident.

One of the first senior policemen at the spot was Superintendent Ernest Barkway, Chief of Essex CID. Mrs French, who must have reported the missing girl to the police was brought to Dedham Road and was able to identify the body as that of Mary Kriek. Mrs French was concerned that she might be obliged to inform Mary's parents, but they were contacted by Interpol. Mary's father Anthonious was a civil servant. He had been celebrating his fifty-third birthday and had recently received a birthday letter from Mary.

A hearse arrived and Mary's rain-soaked body was lifted into it and taken to the mortuary of the Essex County Hospital where a post mortem was performed on Monday by London Hospital pathologist Dr Colin Corby. The cause of death was head injuries inflicted with a heavy blunt instrument, such as a wrench, tyre lever or spanner.

Senior detectives from police headquarters at Chelmsford, under Chief Detective Inspector Peter Clarke, set up an enquiry team at Colchester police station working in collaboration with Colchester CID Chief Detective Inspector George Kemp, Divisional

The body of Mary Kriek is taken away. (By kind permission of Newsquest Essex)

A policeman and detective lay a tarpaulin over the spot where the body was found. (By kind permission of Newsquest Essex)

The men who found the body of Mary Kriek. (By kind permission of Newsquest Essex)

The men leading the hunt for Mary Kriek's killer. (By kind permission of Newsquest Essex)

THE FRENCH FARM

Dr Brady drives away from Bullbanks Farm after treating Mrs French for shock. (By kind permission of Newsquest Essex)

Superintendent Arthur Simpson, head of Colchester police, and Superintendent Barkway. Barkway later presided over a press conference at Colchester police station. He said that the police were very anxious to interview anyone who had seen Mary after she got off the bus. They also wanted to trace her missing shoulder bag, which was made of brown suede with a zip fastener top and a zipped pocket on the side, and contained 'the usual female requisites and a small amount of money.' Her small weekend case had been found beside the body but yielded no clues. Mary was described as 5ft 6in tall and wearing, amongst other things, a blue grey coat of tweedy material, pink headscarf, green cardigan, blue sleeveless blouse, nylon stockings and black court shoes.

All the passengers on the number 88 bus were interviewed. A woman had alighted at the same bus stop as Mary but had then entered her home nearby and did not see where Mary had gone. The stop was about 200 yards from Bullbanks Farm.

House-to-house enquiries commenced at Aldham, Eight Ash Green and Boxsted. A woman told the police she had seen a girl of Mary's description walking down Halstead road with a servicemen and this switched the emphasis of the enquiry to both British and American air bases. Police toured public houses with pictures of Mary, asking, 'have you seen this girl, perhaps with a serviceman?'

By Tuesday the coverage of air bases had spread to East Anglia. The murder weapon was still missing and on Tuesday, soldiers from the Roman Way camp were called out with mine detectors to search near the bus stop and also where the body was found. Unfortunately it was not known where the murder had taken place. It seemed probable that the girl had not been killed where she was found, but had been murdered elsewhere, and her body transported to Dedham Road in a vehicle, and thrown into the ditch. The only clue that emerged was a partial tyre print near where the body was found. The police questioned workers from the nearby farms, asking if they had seen a vehicle in the neighbourhood.

On Wednesday 8 January, Mary's father and sister arrived in England and were met at Harwich by the Fearons and driven to Pear Tree Farm. On the way they were pursued by five or six cars driven by journalists anxious to take photographs. Fearon stopped at one point and asked them to have some regard to the feelings of the distressed relatives, but this did not deter them.

Wherever the murder site was, both it and the killer had to have been liberally spattered with blood. It was thought possible that Mary had been murdered in a car, and on Monday and Tuesday the police checked all the military and civilian vehicles at army and air force bases in Suffolk and Essex for bloodstains, the search extending as far as RAF Wethersfield and Bentwaters. Dry cleaners and laundries were visited to see if bloodstained clothes had been handed in.

The search for the missing bag became more urgent when Willy told the police that Mary carried a scarlet diary in which she had recorded the names of people she had suggested that Mary contact when she came to England.

The savagery of the attack suggested that a deranged killer might be on the loose and possible links with other similar crimes were investigated. Two 17 year old girls had recently gone missing; Ann Noblett, who was last seen at Harpenden, Hertfordshire, about sixty miles away, on 30 December and Isabelle Cooke, who had disappeared in Lanarkshire on 28 December. Both were feared to be murder victims.

The inquest opened at the Orpen Memorial Hall, West Bergholt on Friday 10 January before the deputy coroner for North East Essex, Mr F.E.M. Puxon. The hearing took only seventeen minutes and no members of the public were present. Willy gave evidence of identification but her father, although in attendance, was not called. Dr Jack Nicholas, pathologist at Essex County Hospital, gave evidence which revealed that Mary had been the victim of a frenzied attack. There were seventeen lacerated wounds on her head, and death had been due to a fractured skull and cerebral haemorrhage. There were bruises and fractures of the small bones of both hands, which showed that Mary had been conscious when the attack was carried

Mary's sister and father arrive for the inquest. (By kind permission of Newsquest Essex)

The Orpen Memorial Hall.

out and had tried to protect herself. The head wounds were on the top and back of the skull, suggesting that she had been attacked from behind, and had tried to cover her head with her hands. The inquest was formally adjourned for three months pending police enquiries.

On 11 January, during a football match between Colchester United and Southend, which was attended by about 10,000 people, a broadcast appeal for information was made by Superintendent Simpson. He particularly wanted to know about any cars that might have been seen in the area north west of Colchester on Sunday 5 January and whether anyone had heard of girls or women being accosted there on or about that day. Following the appeal a team of detectives waited in the old supporters club hut ready to interview anyone who might come forward, but no one did.

On 12 January, what was described by the *Colchester Gazette* as 'the biggest comb out ever to take place in Essex' was carried out by 100 uniformed police and CID officers, who questioned 8,000 people in a dawn-to-dusk house-to-house enquiry. The object was to question all the householders in the 80-mile area between the Halstead road at Eight Ash Green and the Ipswich road to establish who was at home on the Sunday night and where they were after 10 p.m. and ask whether they had seen anything suspicious. At Foxes Corner, near the spot where Mary had left the bus, motorists, cyclists and pedestrians were stopped by the police, who also climbed aboard the number 88 bus to question the passengers. All were asked the same question, 'Were you here at this time last week?' Police rest days were cancelled and extra men were drafted in from other divisions in the county to carry out the enquiry. In the week that followed the murder, most of the twenty detectives working at the Colchester murder hunt headquarters were working sixteen hours a day.

The murder weapon had still not been found, and the Essex river police from Tilbury were brought in to search rivers with magnetic drags. When this was unsuccessful they switched their attention to all the ponds, streams and waterways the killer could have passed on his way from Eight Ash Green to Boxsted. It was calculated that there were twenty-four possible routes he could have taken.

Foxes Corner.

Three days after the murder, the police learned of a possible location where the crime had taken place. Mr Wallace Lupino, brother of the musical comedy star Lupino Lane, was licensee of the Wooden Fender public house at Ardleigh, which lay east of Colchester and only a mile and a half from where Mary's body was found. He remembered that at about 1.10 a.m. on the night of the murder he was woken up by a girl's screams. 'They lasted about half a minute and sounded as though they came from the car-park at the side of the house,' he later told the press. 'They were blood-curdling'. He added that he had not connected them with the murder because he was used to getting 'lots of fellows and girls' giggling and screaming and he didn't take any notice of it. It wasn't until 8 January that he and his wife realised that they might have heard something other than a courting couple, and contacted the police. Unfortunately, any traces of the crime that might have remained had been washed away by rain.

Another potentially promising clue was a sighting of a distinctive looking car which had been standing outside Hill House, Aldham, about 100 yards from Foxes Corner. This was seen in the moonlight by farm foreman Albert Britton, who described it as a large two-toned American type car with a fawn or cream top and a blue bottom. The car had no connection with anyone in Hill House. Extensive enquiries were made at British and American service bases but the owner could not be traced.

On the morning of Saturday 11 January, under a leaden sky and sharp, chill showers of driving rain, Mary Kriek was buried at Colchester cemetery. Plain-clothes detectives watched the cortège, which was led by a uniformed police sergeant. The mourners following the hearse included Mary's father and sister, Mr and Mrs Fearon,

Mr and Mrs French and their maid, and some Dutch friends of Mary's. There were eleven wreaths including five from the Netherlands, and one from the police. Renate was not at the funeral. The service was conducted by the Revd Warwick Bailey, who said, 'Every Englishman, and particularly those of us who live in this district, had a sense of shame at the thought of this tragedy.' A photographer took colour pictures during the service so they could be taken back to Holland for the Kriek family. Anthonious Kriek was later reported as saying, 'I have no bitterness for England because I have lost my daughter here. I have no bitterness for the murderer.' After the funeral the Krieks were driven back to Pear Tree Farm in the Fearons' vintage Rolls-Royce.

On Monday 13 January, the police still no nearer to solving the murder, a joint meeting was held at Scotland Yard of all the CID and uniformed branch chiefs involved with the case. Renate's parents had, not surprisingly, asked her to return home, but before she left on 16 January, she had another four-hour interview with the police and gave the names of people Mary had met at English classes and meetings of the International Friendship League. An important fact that emerged was that on the Sunday night Mary had not alighted from the bus at her usual stop, which was about 200 yards from the farm on the Colchester side. The girls had been so immersed in their conversation that Mary missed her stop and the conductor, seeing them sitting together, came up and told Mary she ought to have got off at the last stop. 'Oh, yes, thank you,' said Mary. The girls arranged to meet again when they next had a day off and Mary left the bus at Foxes Corner, waving goodnight to her friend. There were two possible explanations for this, the most probable one being that it was a mistake, and Mary simply missed her stop. It was also theorised that Mary had a secret rendezvous with an unknown person, but there was no evidence to support this romantic notion,

The Wooden Fender.

The grave of Mary Kriek.

and the police doubted it because Mary, who was a reliable girl, knew she had to be back at the farm at a certain time. Renate was reported as saying, 'She had no boyfriends in England and she had only been out of the farm about five times. I was her best friend in England and I know that she was a very nice, quiet, quite religious girl.'

The bus driver, Mr Bertie James French, recalled that when Mary had got off the bus at Foxes Corner she had looked confused about what direction to walk, first of all facing Halstead and then turning around to the direction of Bullbanks. The woman who got off the bus at the same time was a Mrs V.M. Sexton of Foxes Corner. She could not be sure but she thought Mary had walked in the direction of Halstead.

A witness came forward saying that a girl matching Mary's description and carrying a weekend case had been seen walking along the Halstead road at the right time, but going away from the farm, in the direction of Earls Colne. When seen, she was about a quarter of a mile from her home. Was Mary meeting someone, or had she become confused after alighting at the wrong stop? It was a bright moonlit night and Bullbanks Farm was a white building. Inspector Clarke doubted that she would have been able to miss it.

On Wednesday the police were following another clue, searching for a man described as 'copper coloured' with a pencil moustache seen kerb-crawling in the Ash Green area on several nights shortly before the murder. On 17 January, leading forensic expert Dr Francis Camps returned from an overseas lecture tour, and was called in to examine the evidence. He conferred with senior detectives, and said that his tests of cloth fibres and earth samples had led him to believe that the killer was a local man. The newspapers (which were now describing Mary as an attractive blonde) reported that Camps had estimated the time of death at midnight. In reality pathologists cannot give such accurate times, so it should be assumed that she probably died between 11 p.m. and 2 a.m. The police also announced that they had ruled out the possibility of any sexual assault on Mary either before or after death. 'She was absolutely unmolested,' a senior officer told the press.

On the following day, the police followed up their marathon quiz of 8,000 people by revisiting the area to see those people who had been out during the first round of questioning. One hundred special constables, led by Colchester jeweller John Cooper, joined the search for the murder weapon. Local people had also been conducting their own informal searches, including a countryman who told police he cycled every day along roads the killer might have taken looking for the bag, examining all the hedgerows and ditches in the area between Eight Ash Green and Dedham. The police interviewed the crews of two Dutch vessels anchored at the Hythe, Colchester on the weekend of the murder, but this revealed nothing.

On 20 January the ongoing search for a murder weapon was impeded by a fall of heavy snow followed by a hard frost, which caused considerable traffic disruption. The police obtained a photograph of a replica of Mary's shoulder bag, which was published in the newspapers, and Mary's letters home, which had been translated into English by the Dutch Department of Justice, were studied in the hopes that they would reveal secrets which would lead to her killer.

On 24 January, the mysterious man with the pencil moustache was traced and eliminated from the police enquiries.

On 31 January, the body of Ann Noblett was found in a wood at Whitwell. Essex detectives conferred with Hertfordshire CID Chief Detective Superintendent Leonard Elwell and Detective Superintendent Richard Lewis of Scotland Yard at Harpenden police station. There were strong similarities between the two cases. Both Ann and Mary were teenage girls who had disappeared from near a bus stop on a lonely country road, and both had almost certainly entered a vehicle. In both cases there was no sign of a struggle and the bodies were fully clothed. Ann, however, had died of asphyxia. Lewis later went to Colchester to study the Kriek papers.

Halstead Road from the direction of Foxes Corner.

The East Suffolk Police, headed by Chief Detective Inspector Eric Crossland, had been assisting in the widespread search for the murder weapon and Mary's handbag, combing the hedgerows and ditches adjacent to all the roads running out of Essex along which the murderer might have driven after leaving the body. A number of objects discovered during the search were handed to Superintendent Simpson and brought back to Colchester for microscopic tests. West Suffolk Police also helped, but reported their search fruitless. Some four weeks after the murder, Barkway told the press, 'we are being held up a little for reports through Interpol from the continent, but we are still hopeful.'

It had not escaped the newspapers that Mary had been murdered on the night of the full moon, but as the next full moon approached on 4 February the police stated in answer to press queries that they were not expecting another attack. The information sought from Interpol was concerning a serviceman who had been posted abroad shortly after the murder. The police were also waiting for replies to further questions they wished to put to Renate, who was back home in Germany. For several weeks the newspapers declared that the wait for information from abroad was the major difficulty holding up the investigation. Ultimately these enquiries came to nothing. No connection was ever established between any other murders and that of Mary Kriek, and neither was any evidence found which suggested that a serviceman might have been involved.

On 17 January, an event occurred which was for a time given more prominence than the murder. A letter from Roger Fearon was published in *The Times* in which he complained in lurid terms about the conduct of the press. 'Within five minutes of the murdered girl's family in Holland being told of her death,' he claimed, 'reporters from well-known British papers had swarmed into their flat, even penetrating to the girl's bedroom, before being thrown out.' His own family had been 'subjected to a ceaseless stream of journalists.' He stated however that the Essex County Police and the Immigration and Customs Authorities at Harwich had all shown 'sympathy and consideration which I have never seen equalled.' Fearon's letter sparked off a stream of letters to *The Times*. A letter from Violet Bonham Carter was published on 21 January, stating:

> Few can have read Mr Fearon's letter last Friday without deep shame and indignation; shame that reporters of the British Press should have been guilty of the actions he describes; indignation that these outrages on common human decency should be allowed by those that have the power to prevent them.

Lady Bonham Carter urged newspaper owners to take action. On 23 January it was announced that Fearon's complaint was to be investigated by the General Purposes Committee of the Press Council. The general secretary, Mr Alan Pitt Roberts, arranged a meeting with Fearon, who agreed to submit a full statement.

On 15 February, Fearon again wrote to *The Times*. He said that as a result of further consultation with Mary's relatives, he had been informed that the phrase 'even penetrating to the girl's bedroom' should be deleted from his original statement.

On 9 April *The Times* published in full the results of its enquiries into the behaviour of the press in the aftermath of Mary Kriek's murder. The Press Council came to the conclusion that while Fearon had acted in good faith, he had made a number of misleading statements. He had alleged that 'reporters from British papers' had swarmed into the Krieks' flat and that no reporters from any other country 'even Holland itself, took part in this disgraceful scramble.' Enquiries had revealed that none of the reporters, who had possibly numbered about six, who entered the Krieks' flat were British. All were Dutch, although some were acting for British papers. They had not been thrown out of the flat, but Mr Kriek had become angry at their intrusion and asked them to leave, which they did. There was no evidence that any of the reporters acted in a way which was 'callous, offensive or unscrupulous.'

It emerged that an English journalist had submitted a report stating, incorrectly, that a detective had questioned Mr and Miss Kriek shortly after their arrival, whereas the detective had in fact questioned only Fearon on that occasion. Fearon had alleged that the reporter had made up the story because of his own refusal to answer questions. The Press Council concluded that the reporter had simply failed to check his facts and made the assumption that the questioning had taken place. Fearon's complaint that his car had been followed by five or six cars as he drove the Krieks to his home was justified, but his account of harassment on the way there was held to be exaggerated. He had also complained that photographers had wanted to take pictures of the Krieks near the mortuary, but several sources confirmed that the family had posed for pictures willingly. The council did, however, condemn the action of photographers who had entered Fearon's garden to take pictures of the Krieks arriving at his house.

The conclusion was that Fearon had failed to substantiate most of his charges, apart from one instance of an inaccurate report and two of badgering intrusion.

The police carry our door-to-door enquiries. (By kind permission of Newsquest Essex)

Meanwhile, the investigation into Mary's murder had gone quiet. The police revisited Bullbanks Farm, and Barkway and Kemp spoke to Mrs French, but she was unable to provide any additional information.

On 27 April the police made a fresh appeal for the driver of the two-toned car to come forward. Superintendent Arthur Simpson told the press '...we are still very anxious to trace the car outside Hill House that night.' The police had made many appeals for the driver to come forward but he had not done so. Simpson added that if the man had not answered the appeal for 'domestic reasons' his confidence would be respected. The police were still trying to trace another vehicle known to be at the spot where Mary's body was found at about midnight that night. One good piece of news was the weekend thaw, which enabled the river police and their magnetic drags to resume their search for the handbag and weapon, still missing despite extensive searches of the whole area between Boxsted and Eight Ash Green.

At the resumed inquest on 30 April, Barkway admitted that police enquiries had revealed nothing. During the 45-minute hearing, the coroner, Mr F.E.M. Puxon, read evidence of the witnesses at the previous hearing. Barkway said that 20,000 people had been interviewed, hundreds of statements taken, 5,000 vehicles and their occupants checked, and mine detectors used. Two hundred police officers had searched every byway from the Bullbanks Farm to the scene of the crime and beyond. Appeals had been made and every possible avenue had been pursued. No evidence had come forth and the investigation was still proceeding. The coroner addressed the jury saying that, 'it is necessary and advisable...that some finality should be reached and some verdict arrived at if only for the purpose of registration.' The jury found that Mary had been murdered by some person or persons unknown and the inquest was closed.

At the beginning of June Mary's parents and sister came to England. They visited Mary's grave, and spent many hours talking to Barkway and Kemp, discussing aspects of her home background. The address at which they stayed was kept a secret and the fact of their visit was not revealed to the press until the family had returned home. Without revealing details of what was discussed, Kemp said 'As a result of these talks it could be that other lines of inquiry might follow.' Whatever lines of enquiry did emerge, if any, led nowhere. The murder of Mary Kriek remains unsolved, the papers still residing in a 'cold case' file of the Essex Police, a file that remains open to this day.

The most probable sequence of events that night was that Mary, having alighted at the wrong bus stop in error, walked in the wrong direction and after a while accepted a lift. The driver took her to the car park of the Wooden Fender, a spot known to be frequented by courting couples, and made sexual advances which she resisted. She may have jumped out of the car and tried to run towards the house, screaming for help. Her abductor, terrified of being found out, pursued and silenced her with savage blows to the head. The first blow may have brought her to her knees and Mary raised her hands to her head for protection while another sixteen blows

The car park of the Wooden Fender.

Dedham Road.

rained mercilessly down. The killer then drove her body to Dedham Road and threw it in the ditch. Any blood spatter in the car park would have been washed away by the heavy rain that night, and by the time police learned of the possible connection of the site with the murder, all traces were gone.

Isabelle Cooke was later found to be a victim of serial killer Peter Manuel, who led the police to her grave. The killer of Ann Noblett was never found.

Roger Fearon, who was about forty at the time of Mary's death, was one of the many men in the vicinity who had been questioned in connection with the murder. He later shocked his neighbours by having an affair with Fritia de Boer, another Dutch girl who worked for him. His marriage was dissolved and he married Fritia in 1960. The first Mrs Fearon and the three children went to live in another part of the village, and Fearon and Fritia left for Australia and settled in Blackburn, a suburb of Melbourne. On 30 May 1961, Fearon telephoned the police and asked them to come to his home. When the police arrived they found the couple dead. Attractive thirty-year-old Fritia had been shot dead by her husband as she lay in bed asleep. He used a .22 rifle he had bought only the day before. A note was found near the bodies asking that they be cremated and the ashes preserved together as 'we desire to be together always – even in death' but the note gave no reason for his actions.

Had the Essex Police back in 1958 suspected Fearon of being Mary's murderer? Melbourne Police theorised that Fritia had been killed because she knew her husband was involved in the murder and had threatened to reveal it. They made a thorough search of Fearon's belongings in the hope of finding evidence to help solve the three-and-a half-year old mystery of the murder of Mary Kriek. Unsurprisingly, they found many newspaper clippings about the crime, but the homicide squad chief, Inspector J. Matthews, later told the press that an extensive search of Fearon's belongings had produced no evidence to link him to Mary's murder.

It is tempting to suppose that timid Mary would only have accepted a lift from someone she knew; however, one of her letters home shows that this was not the case. In this letter Mary told her parents that she had once got lost on her way back to the farm, but had arrived safely after accepting a lift from strangers.

10

SLEEPING DEATH

Great Dunmow, 1960

On the morning of Tuesday 3 January 1961, the body of a young woman was found beside the A604 (nowadays the A1017) Haverhill to Halstead road, Oaker Hill, near the village of Ridgewell. No attempt had been made to hide the body, which was in a lay-by, with the head in a rain-filled ditch. Officers of the Essex Police, including Detective Chief Superintendent Barkway, Detective Chief Inspector Harry Burden, and Detective Inspector Jeavons, were called to the scene and pathologist Francis Camps examined the body before it was removed to the mortuary at St Michael's Hospital, Braintree. The young woman was wearing a white linen blouse and black gabardine skirt, with a black brassiere and pink nylon panties, but no shoes, stockings or outer clothing. There were scratches and bruises around her neck, and small bruises on her head, the right hip and inner right thigh. There was also a bruise on her left forearm as if it had been tightly gripped. Her hair had been recently and inexpertly cut very short.

Camps determined that the cause of death was 'asphyxia due to compression of the neck ...consistent with manual strangulation.' A mobile police office was set up in the lay-by and a police canteen served hot tea to officers on duty, who stopped all traffic on the road and questioned drivers, while reporters and press photographers swarmed around the scene. Detectives visited all the cafés, shops and public houses in the district asking if anyone had seen the dead girl, but they were unable to identify her.

Later that day Mrs Frances Constable, of 20 Abels Road, Halstead, read about the discovery in her evening newspaper. She had last seen her eldest daughter Jean between 2 and 2.30 p.m. on New Year's Eve. Jean had told her mother she was going to a party in London with some girl friends. 'Don't worry, Mum,' she had said, 'I shall look for a job in London.' Jean had been known to stay out with friends before so her parents had not reported her missing. Even so, they must have been growing

DCS Barkway, front row centre, with DCI Burden to his right. (Courtesy of Essex Police Museum)

anxious because Mrs Constable went to the police. That evening, she was taken to the mortuary where she identified the body of her daughter. Apart from the outer clothing, the girl's handbag was missing, as was her gold watch and a snake ring.

Jean Sylvia Constable was born in Chelmsford on 25 May 1940. Her father, Cecil, worked as a finisher at Lake and Elliott's engineering company, Braintree. Jean was educated at Halstead Secondary Modern School, and had had a variety of jobs, first as a waitress and then at Courtauld's Mill, Halstead. At the time of her death she was living with her parents and sixteen-year-old brother, Dennis, and was working at a plastics factory, Thames Valley Moulders Ltd of Woolpack Lane, Bocking. An attractive, vivacious girl with dark curly hair framing her face, Jean compensated for her humdrum working day with her busy social life. She liked dancing to rock 'n' roll music, and enjoyed the company of young American airmen from the nearby base at Wethersfield. A former RAF wartime airbase, Wethersfield provided facilities for the United States Air Force as part of Britain's NATO commitment, and was home to the 20th Tactical Fighter Wing.

As darkness fell on the first day of the investigation, the headquarters was moved to Braintree. A picture quickly emerged of Jean's movements on New Year's Eve. She had not, as she had told her parents, gone to London. Veronica Benfield, who worked with Jean, had seen her drinking at the Bell public house, Braintree, between 10.30 and 11 p.m. on 31 December. The girl was not drunk, but 'tiddly' and in high spirits. Veronica said that, 'Jean was laughing, giggling, and her eyes sparkled.' She had left the pub with an American airman but Veronica didn't think she would be able to identify him.

On Wednesday the police went to Wethersfield to question the airmen. John William Smith, a second class airman, had been in the Bell that night. He knew Jean and told the police that he had seen her leaving the pub with two men, an airman in the uniform of a staff sergeant, and a civilian.

When Detective Sergeant Johnson spoke to Staff Sergeant Willis Eugene Boshears, he noticed that the airman had a small bruise under his left eye and a recent graze by the side of the eye. Johnson asked Boshears where he had received the injuries and he replied, 'I don't know.'

Soon afterwards, Boshears was interviewed by Detective Inspector Jeavons. Twenty-nine-year-old Boshears, a 5ft 7in wirily built man with black hair, his normally handsome features sunken after recent tooth extractions, admitted that he had known Jean and had met her and her 'boyfriend' in the Bell on 31 December. He had been drinking whisky and beer chasers but, because of his sore gums, had had almost nothing to eat that day. Boshears told the police that the couple had returned with him to his flat for more drinks, and that after an hour or two of drinking vodka he had 'passed out' and awoken the following morning to find that his two guests had gone.

Jeavons, his suspicions already aroused by the unexplained scratches, said that he was not satisfied with this story, and told Boshears that he believed he was the last person to see Jean alive. Boshears hesitated. 'I may as well tell you the truth,' he said. Jeavons cautioned him and he made a full statement. He then handed the policeman Jean's wristwatch and a 10s note he had taken from her handbag. Boshears

The scene where the body was found, January 1961.

was arrested, and taken to Braintree police station, where he was charged with the murder of Jean Constable.

Staff Sergeant Willis Eugene Boshears was born in Detroit Michigan in 1931. His parents William and Lila Boshears divorced when he was less than a year old and he was brought up by his mother, who later remarried. After school in Michigamme, he worked in hotels before joining the USAF in 1949. He served in Japan from January 1950 as a tail gunner, flying forty-nine missions in Korea, mostly with air sea rescue, and returned to the US in May 1952, where he re-trained as a jet engine mechanic. He was awarded the Air Medal with two oak leaf clusters, the Korean campaign and United Nations service ribbons, the National Defence service medal, the Occupation of Japan service medal, the Good Conduct medal, the Republic of Korea Presidential Unit Citation, and the USAF Distinguished Unit Citation with oak leaf clusters.

His next tour of duty was in Prestwick, Scotland, where he arrived in June 1953. There, he met Jane Cunningham. Jane, born on 17 October 1935, was the daughter of a boilerman. She lived with her family at 50 Mill Street and worked as a carpet spooler. Willis Boshears and Jane Cunningham were married at Prestwick on 7 August 1954, and in October they went to live in America where their two daughters Rona and Rhonda were born.

In August 1958 Boshears was transferred to Wethersfield, where he worked as an engineer fitter with the 20th Field Maintenance Squadron. The family occupied a flat about ten miles from the base, at 4 the Close, Great Dunmow, the historic Essex village associated with the flitch ceremony. They were due to return to the US in July 1962.

When Jane was expecting their third child she decided that she would like to give birth in Scotland, and in August 1960 she went to stay with her family in Ayrshire. George Boshears was born in October and two months later, Jane and the children were still in Scotland. Jane was notified of her husband's arrest and reported to the US air base at Prestwick, where she was seen by welfare and legal branch officers.

In Boshears' second statement he told the police that he had known Jean Constable since about September, and she had been to his flat once before, although he had never been alone with her. On 31 December, he had been drinking steadily all day and had had no food since 11 a.m. At the flat that night, he had been drinking vodka and listening to the radiogram while Jean had been having intercourse with her civilian companion on his bed. He later provided a mattress for Jean to sleep on in front of the fire in the lounge. Jean, who was naked, wrapped herself in a blanket and lay down on the mattress to sleep, then Boshears and the 'other fellow' had had more drinks. 'I must have fallen asleep – not fallen asleep but passed out,' said Boshears. He recalled the 'fellow' waking him and asking where he could get a taxi, then leaving. Jean was still asleep and he lay down beside her, and slept. 'The next thing I remember was something scratching and pulling at my mouth. I opened my eyes, and Jean was lying there under me and I had my hands round her throat; she was dead then.' The shock of this discovery sobered him up. He washed and dressed the body and put it on the

The Bell, 1961. (By kind permission of the Essex Chronicle Media Group Ltd)

floor of the bedroom then lay down and slept on the mattress again. In the morning his first thought was that his memory of the terrible events had all been a dream, but when he looked in the bedroom he saw Jean's body. He was too scared to go to the police and the body had lain in the flat until Monday night, when he finally decided to take action. He cut her hair short with scissors, hoping that this would prevent her being identified, and burnt her handbag, fur coat, shoes, stockings, suspender belt and garter. At 11.30 p.m. he wrapped the body in his heavy winter clothes and carried it downstairs to the back of his car, then, after driving around, he found the lay-by and left the body in a ditch. He kept her gold watch and 10s note but threw the snake ring out of the car window. 'I don't know how it all came about' he said. 'I don't know what happened or why I did it.'

The police went to the Dunmow flat, where they found that blankets and towels had been recently washed. In a coal scuttle there were ashes, the metal parts of a handbag, hair slides and a suspender belt. There was a made-up bed on the lounge floor, on which the police discovered cut head hairs. Cut hair was also found in the main bedroom, in the dust bag of the vacuum cleaner and on the back seat of Boshears' Ford car registration 4278 TW. The hair matched samples taken from Jean's body.

The upstairs flat, number 5, was occupied by USAF Sergeant Miller and his wife Clara, who were questioned by the police. Clara said that on 31 December Boshears had handed her his key and asked her to keep his fire going while he was out. He had called to collect the key on his return. Later she heard the sound of music being

The lay-by near Ridgewell.

The Close, Great Dunmow.

played very loud in flat 4 and had thumped on the floor to get him to quieten it down. Eventually her husband went downstairs to complain and the music was turned down. At about 1.30 a.m. Clara heard what sounded like crying from the flat below. Someone was saying either 'You don't love me' or 'You do love me' – she was unable to determine which. When she next saw Boshears she asked him who was crying. 'Was it you Bill?' she asked, but he made no reply.

On 4 January, twenty-year-old apprentice engineer David Sault read the newspaper report of the finding of Jean's body and went to the police. He said he had met Jean for the first time at about 6.30 on the evening of 31 December at the Nags Head, Braintree. She was drinking gin and lime. They had left the pub together at about 9.30 and went to the Bell, where Jean introduced him to Boshears. They had travelled to the flat by taxi, and he freely admitted he had been hoping to sleep with the girl. After dancing to the radiogram and drinking vodka and lime, Boshears had left the lounge to get a mattress and blankets to make up a spare bed. Sault said that Jean had then made advances to him and they had intercourse. They were disturbed by Boshears' return and went into the bedroom, where they had intercourse again. Jean, who was now completely naked, was drowsy and drunk. She went into the bathroom and vomited, then returning to the lounge, rolled herself up in a blanket and lay down on the mattress. Sault, who was partly undressed, lay down beside her, and Boshears also undressed and lay on the floor nearest to Jean. Sault had been intending to stay the night but changed his mind, and got up and dressed. He asked Jean if she wanted to stay there or leave with him, and Jean sleepily replied that she was staying. Boshears told Sault where he could get a taxi to take him home, and, Sault believed, was eager to see him leave.

The police had traced taxi driver Donald Mills, who had driven Boshears, Jean and Sault to the Dunmow flat on 31 December. He recalled the conversation in the back of the car, which seemed to dwell almost entirely on what the sleeping arrangements would be at the flat. Jean had said that she would sleep with the civilian in the GI's bed while the GI would sleep in the other room by the fire.

Boshears spent the night of 4 January at Braintree police station and at 4 p.m. the following day he made his first court appearance at Castle Hedingham magistrates' court. Crowds of air force personnel, press photographers, reporters and the public were waiting when he arrived in a police car.

The officials of the tiny courtroom had to make special arrangements to seat witnesses, public and press. Thirty reporters piled into the small court, which normally had accommodation for only three, and nearly thirty more failed to get in. Boshears, dressed in a denim flying jacket with a fur collar and denim trousers with black laced boots, stood for the whole of the seventeen-minute hearing. Also in court were Colonel E. Dedera, Boshears' squadron commander and Technical Sergeant James D. Geiger from the judge advocate's office at Wethersfield.

Detective Inspector Jeavons gave evidence of arrest, stating that it was not intended to put the accused's statement in as evidence at that stage. The chair of the magistrates' bench, Lady Beatrice Plummer, asked Boshears if he had any questions, and he shook his head and said 'no.' Although the prisoner was American, under British law, when a crime is committed against a British national, the local jurisdiction takes precedence. Nevertheless, the USAF was hoping to deal with the matter under US military law. When Superintendent Wood of Braintree applied for a remand in civil custody, Major Karl Prestin, USAF Staff Judge Advocate, put forward an application for Boshears to be remanded into military custody and held at the air base. Superintendent Wood made a formal objection and Lady Plummer, after conferring with her fellow magistrate Mr Fred Sale, remanded Boshears in civil custody until 13 January.

Boshears was asked if he wanted to make an application for legal aid, and replied that this had already been offered by the US air force. He stepped from the court using his parka jacket to shield his face from the ranks of cameramen, and was taken by car to Brixton Prison.

When the hearing closed, Detective Superintendent Barkway issued a statement recording his appreciation and personal thanks to the members of the public and the press for their co-operation. He also thanked Captain Garry N. Harrell, Provost Marshall of the USAF Wethersfield, his deputy Lieutenant Ernest Teichman and their staff, who 'worked night and day with the Essex police officers in the investigation.'

The inquest on Jean Constable opened on Friday 6 January at Halstead, before acting North Essex coroner Mr F.E.M. Puxon. Cecil and Frances Constable were in court with sixteen-year-old Dennis. When Jean's clothing was described, Frances broke down into sobs and had to be comforted by her husband. The hearing was adjourned until the criminal proceedings had been concluded.

The funeral of Jean Constable took place at the tiny Parkfields Baptist Church, Halstead on Tuesday 10 January. Wreaths were sent by the directors and staff of Thames Valley Moulders. The USAF, as a standard procedure, requested the Director of Public prosecutions to waive primary jurisdiction, so that the case could tried by an American court-martial rather than a British civil court, but the application was rejected. Boshears was not in court at the next hearing on 13 January as he was in the hospital block of Brixton Prison, being treated for influenza, but Major Prestin was there to watch proceedings on his behalf. Lady Plummer remanded Boshears until 20 January.

Boshears was able to appear at Castle Headingham magistrates' court on 20 January, where, defended by Mr Francis Irwin, he pleaded not guilty and reserved his defence. The prosecution was led by Mr Edmund G. MacDermott.

Francis Camps told the court that asphyxiation had been caused by 'a moderate amount of force' and that death may have occurred in 'a matter of seconds', certainly under half a minute.

After hearing fifteen witnesses, the magistrates committed Boshears for trial at the next Essex Assizes at Chelmsford. On 21 January, Jane Boshears returned from Scotland, leaving the children in the care of her mother. In Brixton Prison, Boshears came under the care and observation of the principal medical office F.H. Brisby, and on 31 January, he was examined by consultant psychiatrist Dr Walter Lindsay

Nags Head.(By kind permission of the landlord)

Neustatter. No evidence was found of any disease or psychiatric disorder.

Boshears told Neustatter and Brisby that he had never had any injuries or illnesses of any significance. He had no history of memory loss, phases of dissociation, sleepwalking or depression. He was, however, an unusually deep sleeper. For many years, he had been in the habit of drinking three or four scotches in the evening and was often quite drunk and had occasional lapses, when he had been told afterwards that he was dancing or telling jokes but could not remember what he had done. Neustatter thought that Boshears' capacity for deep sleep and the fact that he had had nothing to eat for most of the day would have made even a regular heavy drinker more susceptible than usual to the effects of alcohol. An electroencephalogram carried out on 7 February resulted in a pattern that was both normal and stable.

The trial opened on Thursday 15 February. Boshears appeared in court in uniform with his medals on his chest and pleaded not guilty. He was represented by Mr V.G. Hines and Francis Irwin, while Mr Stanley Rees QC and Peter Boydell appeared for the Crown.

The defence was one of the most unusual ever to be offered in a court of law, and was at the time unique in British law. Boshears was claiming that he was innocent of murder because he had killed Jean Constable while he was asleep.

Jane Boshears arrived at the court, using her coat to shield her face from the crowds of waiting cameramen. The defence made it clear that there was no estrangement between the couple and Jane was standing by her husband. She and the children had been in Scotland in December only because of arrangements made for the birth of the couple's third child.

The most important witness was David Sault, who said that when the three had left the Bell, Boshears was 'pretty well sober', Jean was merry and he himself had had quite a quantity of whisky and some stout. Mrs Clara Miller told the court of the sobbing noises, which had been 'muffled as though she was holding a handkerchief.'

Mr Rees, cross-examining Francis Camps, referred to the statement made by Boshears about how he had awoken with his hands around Jean's throat. 'On the findings which you made on that body, did you think it is possible that he could have killed her while asleep in that way?'

Camps replied, 'I should think it is certainly within the bounds of improbability. My reason from my findings is this process would take a certain amount of time and during that period the person would go through certain phases of movement and from the

DI Jeavons, third from the left. (Courtesy Essex police museum)

description given of finding her suddenly dead like that I don't think it fits in with that type of death.' Cross-examined by Mr Hines, he admitted that he would not go so far as to say that it was impossible. The trial was adjourned to 16 February when Boshears, the only witness for the defence, took the stand. He was there for an hour and twenty-five minutes.

Boshears said he had slept alone at the flat on 30 December and went to the base the next morning to collect his pay. He had an egg for breakfast and some beer, but was unable to eat any more because of his sore gums. He bought a bottle of vodka and returned to the flat at 1.30 p.m., where he stoked up the fire and had some more drinks. There was no food in the flat at all. He left the flat at about 5 to 5.30 p.m. asking Mrs Miller to keep the fire going, then hitch-hiked to Braintree. There he carried on drinking, first at the Bell, then the Boars Head and later returning to the Bell, where he met Jean.

He told the court that he didn't know how Jean Constable had died:

> There was no quarrel or argument. At no time did I make any overtures of sexual rela-
> tions to her. Nor did I have any desire to kill her or harm her in any way. I cannot throw
> any light on how I came to have marks on my face. I have no more knowledge of how
> Jean met her death than I have told the police and the jury.

He admitted that he had been very much affected by the drink, and had lain beside Jean on the mattress in front of the fire. Questioned about what clothes, if any, they were wearing at the time, he said he wasn't sure. 'I went to sleep almost immediately,' he said. The next thing he remembered was being awoken by something pulling at his mouth. He found that he was on top of Jean, with his hands around her throat and that she was dead. He denied he had quarrelled with Jean or that he had made sexual advances to her. Mr Rees attacked his story. 'The truth is you had a quarrel with the girl soon after Sault left. The girl was crying and sobbing?'

'I don't know.'

'The truth is you wanted intercourse and there was difficulty about that. And you took her by the throat and you killed her?'

'I don't know.'

'And you were wide awake?'

'No, Sir.'

In his final speech to the jury, Rees put forward a simple explanation of what had occurred. 'She cried, and she was heard. And he silenced her. And she died.' Hines told the jury that to constitute murder not only must the killing be a voluntary one, but it must be with malice. 'Unless this man killed that girl when he was not asleep he cannot be convicted of murder,' he said. Hines suggested that it was Jean who had wanted sex with Boshears and he was too sleepy and drunk to respond, and she had been upset. He pointed out that there was no evidence of a struggle, and the lack of any motive was evidence for the girl's death having been accidental.

In his summing up, Mr Justice Glyn-Jones described the case as 'a simple and sordid one' and told the jury that it all came down to the believability of the defendant's story. If Boshears had strangled Jean in his sleep, then it was not a voluntary act and he was entitled to be acquitted. If the jury was in any doubt as to whether he was asleep or not, then he was also entitled to be acquitted. If however they were satisfied that his story must be rejected, then he should be convicted. 'Have you ever heard of a man strangling a woman while he was asleep?' he asked the jury. 'Does there exist any record that such things happen?' From this comment it must have been apparent to the jury that the case was making legal history, for if there had previously been a similar case it would surely have been mentioned. Glyn-Jones also asked if it was 'reasonably within the bounds of possibility that Boshears could have moved away from his position beside the girl, moved any covering which might have been on him, removed the blanket which was covering the girl, arranged himself so that he was lying sprawled on her, and then could have extended his hands, applied pressure and continued to apply it while she passed through the stages to death without his having been awakened either by his own exertions or by her struggling.' He told the jury to 'use your common sense.'

The jury of eleven men and one woman retired at 3.32 p.m. While Jane Boshears awaited the verdict, she was, according to a report in the *Modesto Bee and Herald News*, approached by Mrs Frances Constable. Mrs Constable said, 'This must be a terrible ordeal for you and your children,' and Jane replied, 'It must be for you, too.' When the jury returned to the court room at 5.21 p.m. to deliver their verdict, Jane could not bring herself to go in.

Willis Boshears was acquitted. The news was greeted with muffled cheers and gasps from the crowded gallery, while the prisoner seemed to sway and look surprised. One of Jane's sisters brought the news to her. 'Bill is acquitted, acquitted.

They've found him not guilty!' Jane broke down and sobbed with relief. 'What happens now?' she asked.

Boshears left the court with some American officers and, on the following day, he and Jane spoke to the press in a small TV lounge at the Wethersfield base community centre. Asked what he thought of British justice he said 'I like it very much', but admitted, 'I was ready for a verdict either way. I had rather resigned myself to the worst.'

The press wanted to know if the couple were reconciled and after a short pause Boshears replied, 'yes, we are going to try to forget the whole unhappy affair' while Jane added, 'I've forgiven Bill because I love him. Now all we want to do is to get away from it all.' Boshears said he hoped to be able to see his children in Scotland before his leave expired.

Boshears was given a three-day pass by his squadron commander so that he could be with his family. He also received a cheque for $800 backpay. An official of USAF Wethersfield told the press that no action would be taken by the American authorities. 'As far as we are concerned he has been acquitted of the charge and that is an end of the matter.'

The unique nature of the Boshears case led to an exchange in the House of Lords on 28 February, when Lord Elton asked the Government whether as a result they were considering bringing about a change in the law to make possible a verdict of 'guilty but asleep'. Earl Bathurst, Under-Secretary for the Home Office, replied, 'From the inquiries I have been able to make it would appear that the circumstances of this case are without precedent. I have no reason to think that it has demonstrated the need for a change in the law.' Lord Elton persisted.

> Would not the Under-Secretary agree that a verdict of 'guilty but asleep' would be much nearer to the facts than a verdict of innocent and would also have the advantage that like a verdict of 'guilty but insane' it would make it possible to detain the convicted person. Would he not agree that when a bizarre case like this has been widely reported it is more than likely that it will either be imitated subconsciously and unwittingly by persons of neurotic temperament or deliberately simulated by persons who desire a plausible line of defence?

'It is true,' replied Earl Bathurst, 'that there might be a possibility that the verdict of 'asleep' might in future be considered to be part of mental disorder and the Home Secretary is looking into that very carefully. Meanwhile I can only say that so far as this is such an extraordinary result of a case, such an extraordinary decision has been made, that for the time being the Home Secretary sees no reason to alter the law.' 'If a man is asleep, how can he be guilty?' asked Lord Amwell, provoking laughter in the House. 'Surely the man was not guilty?' said Lord Derwent, 'he was found not guilty.' 'That is right,' said Earl Bathurst. 'The point Lord Amwell brought up is the conundrum we are faced with.'

Lord Ogmore questioned whether it was proper for a minister of the Crown to describe the verdict as 'extraordinary' and Viscount Hailsham observed that he was

Left *Willis E. Boshears in 1961. (By kind permission of the Essex Chronicle Media Group Ltd)*

Right *David Sault in 1961. (By kind permission of the Essex Chronicle Media Group Ltd)*

sure that Earl Bathhurst did not wish to question the verdict of the court. The Earl apologised if he had used the wrong term, but Lord Elton commented, 'It would not have been possible to use a more appropriate word. It was a case out of the ordinary.' The last word went to Lord Stonham. 'Can the Minister give an assurance that when they are tried at the bar of public opinion for their many lapses, the Government will not put in a plea of "guilty but asleep?"', and with the laughter of the House the debate ended.

A page 1 editorial in the *Essex Chronicle* of 3 March referred to the many letters that readers had sent in on the subject. 'All of them express astonishment at the verdict, which has made legal history in this country. The matter has been raised in the Commons and in the House of Lords. Never before has there been a similar case. Other readers express anger, indignation, or disgust.' All expressed sympathy for the bereaved family. Mrs Constable had also written to the paper. It is a bitter, bewildered document in which she says she was 'amazed and shocked by the jury's decision.' The editor asked for readers to contribute to a fund for the family's unpaid bills for the funeral expenses.

Boshears had had to give up the Dunmow flat on his arrest. After a three-day break with his family he entered hospital at the USAF HQ for a check-up, and his extensive dental work was completed. He was then transferred to another USAF hospital for psychiatric study, but it was later announced that there was no question of his receiving psychiatric treatment.

The USAF transferred Boshears and his family to the air force base at Glasgow Montana, and on Wednesday 8 March they flew back to the USA. Boshears left a statement with the public information office. 'I have nothing to say and want to forget the whole thing.'

Willis, Jane and their children settled in Michigamme. Another son, Charles, was born in 1962. Jane, usually nicknamed 'Scotty', worked in the bar and restaurant business, and took an active role in community events. She never lost her Scottish accent and over the years made several trips to Scotland to see her family. Jane died on 10 December 2003 and her obituary in *The Daily Mining Gazette* of 4 January 2004 stated that she was survived by her husband of forty-nine years, four children, eleven grandchildren and five great-grandchildren.

The deliberations of the jury in the Boshears case must always remain confidential so one can only speculate on how they arrived at their verdict. The judge's scepticism might have worked both for and against the defendant. Glyn-Jones had emphasised the improbability of the defence's claim but on the other hand, the jury having no similar case to compare it with, had nothing as a reference point. Had there been other such cases they would have been able to judge Boshears' claims against proven cases of automatism, and see what features they had in common. All they could do was apply their own judgement. One possible scenario the jurors might have discussed was that Boshears, sexually frustrated by the long absence of his wife, further overwrought both by alcohol and having to listen to Jean and David Sault having intercourse only yards away, finally found himself alone with Jean for the first time, and gave in to his instincts. Jean, sleepy and drunk, and having had sex twice already and then been sick, could well have resisted.

Before them, the jury saw a young war veteran with medals pinned to his chest and a loyal Scottish wife, the mother of his three small children. Understandably, they might well have felt unwilling to condemn him on the basis of a decision about the complex workings of the human mind, about which none of them had the expertise to feel confident. Reasonable doubt alone was enough to secure an acquittal.

But what actually did happen that night? How did Jean die? Was Boshears asleep when it happened? And why did he offer such an unusual defence? The psychiatric reports provide some clues which may bring us closer to the truth.

There is no evidence that Willis Boshears had any intention of harming Jean Constable, however he had freely admitted that he was lying on top of Jean when she died, and had also told Neustatter that during his wife's absence, 'he felt very lost without her and once or twice had extramarital relations.' Some attempt at intercourse may have taken place which Jean resisted. Knowing that sounds could carry to the upstairs flat, he may have attempted to quieten her. Dr Neustatter did not believe that Boshears had killed Jean in his sleep but stated that in a man who was, like Boshears, normally a very deep sleeper, alcohol could have had more of an effect than usual. Boshears had been drinking steadily that day and had had very little food. Under the effects of alcohol he could have become confused and unable to judge how much force he was exerting when he tried to quieten Jean, and unintentionally strangled her.

Although he may not actually have been asleep when Jean died, he might genuinely have thought he had been. Not only did he have a history of not recalling things he had done while drunk, there is also another possible element – amnesia resulting from shock. Dr Brisby believed that Boshears' impairment of memory for the critical time was partly due to alcohol, with 'possibly an element of repression of a painful episode.' Neustatter also stated that the memory loss might have been due to shock. If the shock of finding Jean dead had made Boshears blank the traumatic events from his mind, it might well have seemed to him that he had awoken from a sound sleep to face a waking nightmare.

BIBLIOGRAPHY

GENERAL

Genealogy records accessed at www.
    ancestry.com www.familysearch.org
    www.1911census.co.uk
The Times
Records of the Essex Police Museum

SPECIFIC REFERENCES

Chapter 1. *In a Dark and Lonely Place*

Anon, *A Full and Particular Account of the trial and Execution of John Pallett on Dec 15th 1823 for the cruel and barbarous murder of Mr James Mumford on Monday Dec 8th near Widdington in Essex,* (Gateshead, W. Stephenson, 1823)

Anon, *The Trial of John Pallett, for the wilful murder of Mr. James Mumford holden at Chelmsford the 13th day of December, 1823,* (Chelmsford, Maggy & Chalk, 1823)

The Chelmsford Chronicle
The Morning Chronicle
The Morning Post
Widdington burial records accessed at the Family History Centre, London, microfilm 1702677

Wilkinson, J., *A Sermon, delivered at the Upper Meeting, Saffron Walden on Sabbath Evening. December 21st, 1823 ... in consequence of* the melancholy, wilful, and cruel murder of Mr James Mumford, (Saffron Walden, G. Youngman, 1824)

Chapter 2. *The Mildness of Murderers*

Anon, *Confession of Thos. Drory,* (London, Disley, 1851)

Anon, *Copy of verses on Drory and Jael Denny,* (London, E. Hodges, 1851)

Anon, *Horrible Murder of Jael Denny, aged 20, at Donninghurst [sic], near Brentwood, in the county of Essex,* (London, publisher unknown, 1850)

Anon, *The lamentation of Thos. Drory, who now lays in Chelmsford Jail, for the murder of Jael Denny, his sweetheart,* (London, Disley, 1851)

Anon, *The Queen v Thomas Drory, The Speech of Edwin James esq on behalf of the prosecution* (London, S. Francis, 1851)

Kurton, Peter, *Doddinghurst a Place in the Country,* (Basildon, 1999, PBK Publishing)

The Essex County Standard
National Archive papers PRO ASSI 36/6

Chapter 3. *The Love Match*

The Essex Standard
National Archive papers, PRO ASSI 36/17
Thorrington baptismal records accessed London Family History Centre microfilm 1702645

Chapter 4. Twice Vexed

The Essex Standard
The Essex County Chronicle
The Essex Weekly News
Lockwood, Martyn, The Murder of Sergeant Eves, (Essex Police History Notebook No.1) accessed http://www.essex.police.uk/museum/history_01.htm
National Archives papers PRO COPY 1/412/141

Chapter 5. 'Where is Florrie?'

Anon, *Southend Crime. Florrie Dennis found shot. Capture of Read at Mitcham.* [Songs.] (Unknown publisher, 1894)
The *Essex County Standard*
National Archive papers
PRO HO 144/261/A56481
PRO MEPO 3/153

Chapter 6. Murder in Honeypot Lane

The *Essex Standard*
The *Essex Herald*
National Archives papers, PRO HO 144/840/146334

Chapter 7. My Darling Girl

National Archive papers
PRO CRIM 1/584/79
PRO CRIM 1/205/3
PRO HO 144/13559
PRO PCOM 8/170
PRO PCOM 8/370
PRO MEPO 3/1576
The Walthamstow and Leyton Guardian
The Essex Herald

Chapter 8. Two Were Hanged

Berry-Dee, C. and Odell, R., *The Long Drop*, (True Crime, London, 1993)
Berrett, Chief Inspector J., *When I was at Scotland Yard*, (London, Sampson Low, Marston & Co Ltd, 1933)
Coniston, W.L., (ed.) *The Gutteridge Murder.*

Report of the trial of Frederick G. Browne and William H. Kennedy., (London, A. Rogers & Co., 1928)
Savage, Ex-Supt. P., *Savage of Scotland Yard,* (Hutchinson and Co, London, undated)
Shore, W. Teignmouth, (ed.), *Trial of Frederick Guy Browne and William Henry Kennedy,* (Edinburgh and London, William Hodge and Company, 1930)
The Oxford Chronicle
National Archive papers PRO MEPO 3/1631
Essex Police Memorial Trust Roll of Honour, accessed http://www.essex.police.uk/memorial/roll_gut.htm
Birth certificate of 'Frederic Guy Brown'

Chapter 9. The Dutch Girl

The *Colchester Gazette*
The *Colchester Express*
The *Daily Mail*
The *Melbourne Herald*
The *Melbourne AGE*
The *Woodford Times*

Chapter 10. Sleeping Death

Essex County Standard
Halstead Gazette
Ironwood Daily Globe, Michigan
Jackson, Robert, *Francis Camps*, (Granada, London, 1983)
National Archive papers PRO ASSI 36/321
Obituary of Jane Boshears in *The Daily Mining Gazette* 4 January 2004, accessed via: www.ancestry.com
The Essex Chronicle
Modesto Bee and Herald News
News-Palladium (Benton Harbor Michigan)
Marriage certificate of Willis Eugene Boshears and Jane Cunningham
MDPGA, Wethersfield, accessed: http://en.wikipedia.org/wiki/MDPGA_Wethersfield (an article incorporating public domain material from websites and documents of the Air Force Historical Research Agency)

INDEX